Open Door to Learning

Open Door to Learning

The Land-Grant System Enters Its Second Century

By Herman R. Allen

University of Illinois Press, Urbana, 1963

Foreword

The year 1962 marked the centennial of a uniquely American institution, the nationwide system of Land-Grant colleges and universities, of which there are now 68, at least one in every state and Puerto Rico.

A centennial is sometimes an awesome, frequently a joyful, always a contemplative occasion. In the lives of most persons, nations, and institutions it calls for some sort of commemoration, and the Land-Grant colleges were no exception. As early as 1957 they began to plan how best to mark the completion of 100 years of vigorous life.

One of the first things they did was to appoint a theme committee to decide a critical question: What was it that they wished to commemorate? The more the committee members [1] pondered the question, the more apparent it became to them that these institutions would not want to commemorate anything in the usual sense. They would not be content simply to rehearse the accomplishments, glorious though these had been, of their first century of life. Rather, they would wish to look ahead, to see how well prepared they were for the challenges of their second century.

Out of this conviction came a theme statement which said in part: "Education faces always the problem that the Land-Grant movement founders discerned a century ago: the requirement for reappraisal, reorganization and redirec-

---

[1] Dr. J. L. Morrill, then president of the University of Minnesota, President David D. Henry of Illinois, Dean Lyman E. Jackson of Pennsylvania State, and President John A. Perkins of Delaware.

v

tion to meet the needs of time and change. Persistence in old patterns, however resourceful and responsive in their day, are not sufficient to the future which becomes the pressing present."

From this broad statement of purpose, in turn, came two specifics: (1) to assess and evaluate the work being done by Land-Grant institutions as they entered their second 100 years of life; (2) to build public understanding of them and what they do.

In furtherance of the first specific, the Centennial Steering Committee, of which I have the honor to be chairman, decided on two procedures. First it would call on "outside" authorities—outside in the sense that they were not connected, at least currently, with the Land-Grant system—to evaluate Land-Grant work in each of eight subject-matter areas. Second, in recognition of the fact that Land-Grant institutions, in larger proportion than any other colleges and universities, were already involved in international educational activities, it would set up four committees to conduct self-studies of this broad theme.[2] The reports of evaluators and study groups were highlights of the Land-Grant Centennial Convocation at Kansas City, Missouri, November 12-16, 1961.

The work of the study groups, as well as other activities of an international flavor during the Centennial Year—the bringing of several noted foreign educators to Kansas City as speakers, for instance—was made possible by a grant from the Carnegie Corporation.

The same grant made it possible to carry out the second specific of the Centennial purpose, to build public understanding, which is the aim of this benchmark volume. It is the hope of the Steering Committee that the reader will not only gain an understanding of the Land-Grant system and its aspirations but will be inspired to look at the Land-Grant institutions in his own state and ask: "How well are

[2] A roster of evaluators and international study group members appears following this Foreword.

we doing in view of what is possible, what is being done, and what is demanded? Are we supporting *our* Land-Grant institutions in what they must do and are attempting to do?"

This, then, is no volume of history. The record of the Land-Grant system has been stated elsewhere. Nevertheless, for the benefit of the reader who may not be entirely familiar with the Land-Grant story, a few essential facts may be useful here.

Credit for devising the Land-Grant system is divided by educational historians between a Vermonter, Justin Smith Morrill, and an Illinois educator, Jonathan Baldwin Turner. There is evidence that Turner spoke of the possibilities of such a system as early as 1851, but it was Morrill who brought it to fruition.

Morrill, who had to leave school at the age of 15, nevertheless became a successful merchant and later entered Congress. Always conscious of the handicaps he had endured because of his lack of education, he introduced in Congress a bill giving each state 30,000 acres of federally owned land in the western states for each of its members of Congress. The land was to be sold and the proceeds invested, with the income to be used to endow instruction at a new kind of college—a college which would "promote the liberal and practical education of the industrial classes in the several pursuits and professions of life." In those days "the industrial classes" meant just about everyone who worked for a living, as distinguished from the elite who pursued the purely classical education offered by the colleges of the time.

The bill was enacted into law after many legislative adventures, including a veto by President Buchanan, and was finally signed by President Abraham Lincoln on July 2, 1862, midway in the Civil War.

The Morrill Act stipulated in return for the federal grant only that the colleges offer instruction in agriculture, in "the mechanic arts" (which we call engineering today), and in military tactics. It also stated, however, that this should be done "without excluding other scientific and classical studies," a provision which means to all Land-Grant institutions that these studies, more generally known today as the liberal arts, be definitely included in their curricula. Thus, while the modern Land-Grant system includes almost all of the nation's colleges of agriculture and many of the leading engineering colleges, it also includes some of the finest liberal arts colleges.

Within this historical framework has been built a higher education responsive both economically and philosophically to the needs and expressed wishes of the American people. I was struck recently by the words of a noted British economist, John Vaizey, who wrote:

> In the U.S.A. . . . it was always a principle of American democracy, and of the reformed religion that was its main impulse, that the people should be well educated; and this was an impulse given an enormous boost after the Civil War by the Land-Grant colleges. All along, too, American education has had as an important job the aim of preparing people to earn their livings—hence the importance of agricultural education, for example. Thus, in America, democratic impulses and the needs of the economy created a skilled and educated population through a mass education system; and consequently America has always tended to spend more of its national income on education than other countries.[3]

Although I should prefer to use the expression "invest more" rather than "spend more," I feel that this is a quite admirable analysis of the underlying attitude toward education in this country. Certainly we do invest heavily in education, and certainly this investment has paid dividends in the thousands of per cents, as our economic status alone —to say nothing of our national health and cultural status —will testify.

Moreover, through prosperity and adversity, our Land-Grant system has maintained an open door for all who can

[3] *The Economics of Education,* The Free Press of Glencoe, New York, 1962.

profit by what it offers. To a man, Land-Grant educators believe that this is as it should be. To us, the words spoken many years ago by former President E. C. Elliott of Purdue are still true: "If the Land-Grant college fails, neither democracy's goal of education nor education's goal of democracy will be reached."

Tucson, Arizona   Richard A. Harvill
October 18, 1962   President, University of Arizona

Divisional Evaluators

Natural Sciences: Dr. Detlev W. Bronk, President, The Rockefeller Institute

Social Sciences: Dr. Bernard Berelson, Director, Bureau of Applied Social Research, Columbia University

Over-all: President Conrad A. Elvehjem, University of Wisconsin (deceased)

HOME ECONOMICS

Dr. Reuben G. Gustavson, University of Arizona

TEACHER EDUCATION

Dr. Lawrence D. Haskew, Vice Chancellor, University of Texas

VETERINARY MEDICINE

Dr. William A. Hagan, Director, National Animal Disease Laboratory, Ames, Iowa

Centennial International Study Groups

I. *The Special Role of Land-Grant Colleges and State Universities in Meeting the Needs of Developing Nations*

Dr. H. W. Hannah, Professor of Agricultural and Veterinary Law, University of Illinois

Dr. Willard M. Fifield, Secretary-Manager, Florida Agricultural Research Institute

Dr. Clifford Liddle, Professor, School of Education, University of Wisconsin

Dr. Erven Long, Specialist in Land Policies and Problems, Agency for International Development

Dr. William Pickett, Campus Coordinator, India-Kansas State University Contract, Kansas State University

II. *Steps Needed to Improve or Develop Programs to Meet the Needs of Foreign Scholars, Students, and Trainees*

Dr. John McConnell, Dean, New York State School of Industrial and Labor Relations, Cornell University (now president of the University of New Hampshire)

Dr. Royden Dangerfield, Associate Provost, University of Illinois

Dr. Raleigh Fosbrink, Professor, School of Agriculture, Purdue University

President Francis H. Horn, University of Rhode Island

Dr. Gerard Mangone, Executive Officer, Maxwell Center for the Study of Overseas Operations, Syracuse University

Dr. Arthur T. Mosher, Executive Director, Council on Economic and Cultural Affairs

Dr. Stewart Patterson, Chief, Education Training Division, Office of Educational Services, Agency for International Development

III. *Education of Americans to Serve Abroad—and of America to an Understanding of This Country's Role in World Affairs*

Dr. Harvey Baty, Director, International Cooperation Center, Montana State College

Dr. Jack Gray, Director, Foreign Programs, Texas A & M College System

President James A. McCain, Kansas State University

Dr. Ralph Smuckler, Associate Dean, International Programs, Michigan State University

Dr. Clarence Thurber, Program Associate, International Training and Research Programs, The Ford Foundation

IV. *How Far Should Government—State and Federal —Go Toward Support of Public Higher Education in International Programs?*

Dr. Harry R. Wellman, Vice President, University of California

President D. W. Colvard, Mississippi State University

President Fred Harrington, University of Wisconsin

Dr. Eldon Johnson, President, Great Lakes College Association, Detroit Metropolitan Airport, Michigan

Summary and Evaluation of Divisional and International Papers

President David D. Henry, University of Illinois

Contents

NOTE: Full texts of evaluation and study group papers, as well as all other papers read at the Kansas City Convocation, were printed in the 1961 *Proceedings of the Association of State Universities and Land-Grant Colleges.* These *Proceedings* are on file at most state university libraries and at some other university and public libraries.

Introduction

Thirty years ago President W. J. Kerr of Oregon State Agricultural College summarized a fourfold Spirit of the Land-Grant Institutions:

1. The spirit of initiative—pioneering;
2. The spirit of growth—progress;
3. The spirit of equal opportunity for all—democracy;
4. The spirit of helpfulness—service.

Although President Kerr, if he were alive today, might scarcely recognize many of the problems faced by what is now Oregon State University, and by the 67 other Land-Grant institutions, the underlying spirit which he delineated can still be applied to those problems as validly as it could to the problems of his own long-vanished America.

Speaker after speaker among the array of thoughtful men who addressed the Land-Grant Centennial Convocation in Kansas City restated its essence with a unanimity that was too great to be simply coincidental. Yet each of these speakers cautioned that—enduring and universal as this spirit might be—it must be interpreted and applied today in accordance with vastly changed conditions. As the historian Allan Nevins put it:

Service to democracy is a phrase which today demands a broader definition than of old. Our principal democratic ideals have been freedom and equality. The state and Land-Grant universities have an ever-sharper responsibility for promoting freedom in inquiry, freedom in the discussion of ideas, and freedom in the dissemination of truth. . . . These institutions have an equal duty, in relation to equality, of keeping our nation an *open* society and a *mobile* society. They have a prime function, that is, in contributing to equality of opportunity, giving every ambitious person, young or old, poor or rich, well-trainied or ill-trained, a chance adapted to his gifts; helping people move freely from position to position, from rank to rank.

And this, Professor Nevins emphasized in a particularly measured sentence, "is far harder today than a century ago."

The gravity of the demands placed upon the Land-Grant system by the foreseeable future was underscored further by Glenn T. Seaborg, chairman of the U.S. Atomic Energy Commission. A onetime self-supporting student at the Land-Grant University of California, who rose to become chancellor of that university's Berkeley campus, Dr. Seaborg said: "For all practical purposes, insofar as our generation is concerned, we are in a state of continuing—or perhaps I should say permanent—crisis. . . . One day, I believe, the world either will be enslaved, or it will be free. . . . If this issue is decided in favor of the forces of freedom —as we must resolve it shall be—it will be largely the result of education and the things the educated can do. The long war of the mind will be won in the classroom, in the libraries, and in the laboratories."

The task confronting universities and colleges, Dr. Seaborg said, is nothing less than to "help preserve and expand our libertarian and humanistic civilization." And, he reminded his audience of Land-Grant presidents, "a significant portion of the program of higher education lies within the tradition and responsibility of the Land-Grant colleges and universities."

How can Land-Grant colleges and universities carry out the injunction of Dr. Seaborg, an injunction reinforced time and time again by other Convocation speakers, that they bring to bear their unique traditions and competencies to "help preserve our libertarian and humanistic civilization?" How can they discharge what Professor Nevins summarized as their "duty of fostering a healthy diversity in intellectual and social life; of encouraging social experimentation; and of nurturing tolerance and liberalism— these being essential to an open society?"

To begin with, of course, the lines that once so sharply distinguished the Land-Grant institutions from other public universities and colleges, and from private ones, have become blurred over the years. President David D. Henry of the University of Illinois, in concluding his brilliant summary of the findings of the Kansas City Convocation, pointed this up when he asked: "Now that the broad philosophy and general purposes of the Land-Grant institutions have been widely adopted by higher education generally . . . is there a characteristic 'Land-Grant' pattern for the future?"

President Henry answered himself by quoting an earlier Convocation speaker, Philip H. Coombs, then Assistant Secretary of State, who had cautioned: "Just as the idea of freedom is not the monopoly of any one nation, so the Land-Grant college idea of practical service cannot and should not be the monopoly of any one type of institution. The Land-Grant colleges can take pride in the fact that their once distinctive characteristic is now being nationalized and internationalized, not as a carbon copy of their particular curriculum, organizational structure and methods but as a compelling idea which can be adapted to appropriate local needs and forms in any nation."

Agreeing in broad principle with Secretary Coombs that the Land-Grant philosophy is a growing trend, President Henry nevertheless recognized that it is still far from universal in American higher education. Thus, he concluded, "the destiny of the Land-Grant institutions lies within the vigor of their leadership in seeking to have *all* of higher education more definitely aligned with the democratic impulses of our time as Turner and Morrill did in theirs."

Meanwhile, what must the Land-Grant institutions, with their own well-developed understanding of these democratic principles, do here and now and in the immediate future to "preserve and expand our libertarian and humanistic civilization"?

Without exception, every speaker at Kansas City, every divisional evaluator, every international study group, projected two broad categories of opportunity through which Land-Grant institutions may help achieve this grand objective: (1) expand their constituencies; (2) widen and deepen their educational offerings.

With respect to the first category, concern was expressed that—without forgetting their historic mandate to minister to the needs of rural people—the Land-Grant colleges and universities take even sharper cognizance of the needs of city dwellers as well. Urban redevelopment was just one problem cited as within the Land-Grant potentiality.

Nor was this by any means all. Consistently throughout the Convocation, the contention of Dr. Seaborg—that a significant portion of what higher education can do to ease the anguish of the world at large "lies within the tradition and responsibility of the Land-Grant colleges and universities"—was restated and re-emphasized. These institutions, many of which are already active in the international area, were urged to descry ways in which they could involve themselves more effectively beyond our American borders and shores. All this, of course, while building at home, on the campus, in order to maintain the open-door doctrine which holds that every student should have the opportunity for education to the limit of his abilities.

With respect to the second category, no area of Land-Grant teaching escaped unscathed in the findings of the "outside evaluators" who over a period of months had put each of the Association's eight subject-matter divisions under the microscope. Vastly greater emphasis on the liberal arts and a build-up in graduate work and research were called for—along with an awakening to modern demands in the fields of agriculture, home economics, veterinary medicine, engineering, and teacher education. A desperate need was documented for general extension on a par in scope and caliber with the cooperative extension which serves the "farm and home" area.

Plainly these two categories fall validly within the Land-Grant spirit enunciated by President Kerr. Plainly, too, however, like the four parts of the spirit which President Kerr listed, they must be considered as one.

To widen and deepen the quality of education without making its fruits available to more people, a larger constituency, would be to deny the very basis of the Land-Grant philosophy itself.

To expand a constituency without offering it the best education devisable would result in intolerable superficiality in an age when worldwide malaise demands deep and sympathetic understanding.

To refine and synthesize still further, then, and to put it in homely terms, what is needed is better education for more people.

True, this challenge could be posed for all education. Yet, with their long-standing tradition of service and opportunity, a large part of the burden will rest on the Land-Grant institutions.

☆

PART ONE

Expanding Constituencies

"Service to democracy," Allan Nevins said at
Kansas City, "is a phrase which today demands
a broader definition than of old." To the Land-
Grant college or university, as indeed to every
public institution of higher learning, this means
basically two things: expansion of its constituency and widening of its educational offerings.
Part One of this volume deals with the first
aspect, the expansion of constituencies, first at
home and second in the developing nations
overseas.

CHAPTER ONE

Opportunities in Urban Areas

To emphasize the situation rather than because it was completely new to their listeners, speaker after speaker at Kansas City made reference to the changing complexion of the American nation.

When the Land-Grant system was born, they recalled, more than half of the population lived on farms, whereas today this figure is less than 10 per cent. Moreover, with the growth of the total population, cities have become both bigger and more numerous.

The consequences of this as far as the Land-Grant system is concerned are essentially two. First, the growth of cities has created concentrations of working adults who need organized programs of higher education, both vocational and liberal, and can be relatively easily reached by them. Second, the cities themselves, as geographic, social, and economic entities, developing haphazardly in some cases, deteriorating in some others, but almost all with growth problems of some sort, challenge the Land-Grant institutions to new applications of their historic tradition of *service*.

To cite the need for educational programs for city-dwelling adults is not to suggest that Land-Grant and other public universities and colleges will in the foreseeable future face any less of a challenge to provide high-grade undergraduate and graduate education on their campuses. The enrollment pressure on these institutions, as on all

9

institutions of higher learning, will continue to be tremendous for a long time to come. The Land-Grant institutions in particular, however, with their tradition of educational opportunity for all who are qualified, have done a good job so far of finding room for every worthy student. Sometimes this has been accomplished under difficulties, but it may be taken for granted that these institutions will continue to meet their responsibilities.

Nor is the need for service to the rural areas by any means vanishing. The rapidly developing necessity for intelligent planning for rural and semirural land use is only one facet of the continuing requirement for service to these areas, in which the Land-Grant institutions are so deeply rooted.

Nevertheless, the burgeoning problems of the city are so great as to demand special examination as a new field of Land-Grant endeavor. The matter of rural activities will be taken up in detail in a later chapter.

It would not be accurate or fair to give the impression that Land-Grant institutions as a whole, or public higher education as a whole, have been indifferent to urban requirements. Splendid starts have been made. One has only to look at the long-standing evening program for adults on the Los Angeles campus of the University of California, for instance, or at the statewide system of "continuing education" centers in Wisconsin, among other states, to see that this is true with respect to educational activities. And the surge of urban affairs projects by Land-Grant as well as other public universities since World War II is evidence that at least some of them are aware of this new area of opportunity for service.

In both the educational and the service areas, it is important to note, thoughtful leaders are thinking in very human terms. It is important to note, too, the extent to which they consider educational and service activities to be interlocked.

Shortly after he had been designated as chancellor of the

still-to-be-built Irvine campus of the University of California, Daniel G. Aldrich, Jr., wrote: "When I was asked to consider the chancellorship I said that I would be interested in the opportunity provided I could carry forward the spirit of the Land-Grant idea on this new campus."

What did Aldrich, who was serving as dean of agriculture of the California university system at the time he was selected for his new post, mean by "the spirit of the Land-Grant idea"? In his words:

> The essence of the Land-Grant idea, as far as I am concerned, is educational opportunity for all qualifying and a vital concern to research and extension education for the needs of society. In attempting to develop the distinctive character for Irvine, I asked myself the question, what are the needs of people in this time? . . . The longer I ponder this question, the more convinced I become that the real problem facing people today is one of how they shall occupy the landscape. All about us we see the consequence of faulty decision-making on the part of people, resulting in the pollution of the atmosphere, pollution of water and pollution of the land resource. . . . I hope that we shall be able to explore at Irvine the interrelations between natural resource utilization and development—open space—and human resource utilization and development—urban space.

Three thousand miles away in distance but side by side with Aldrich in conviction, President Mason W. Gross of Rutgers, the Land-Grant state university of New Jersey, was making a speech at very nearly the same time Aldrich was writing.

Addressing the National Conference on Urban Life, which Rutgers sponsored as a contribution to observance of the Land-Grant Centennial, President Gross said: "I propose that we think of the city as the outward expression of the thoughts, sensations, emotions and values of its inhabitants, past and present. In these terms we may think of a happy and successful city as the fulfillment of the thoughts and aspirations of its inhabitants, and a declining city as one in which the emotional impulses are thwarted, frustrated, diluted or cancelled out. . . . A city is in good shape when its inhabitants enjoy living there, and in bad shape when they want to move out."

In inquiring into why "all too many of the inhabitants" of our cities want to move away, Gross highlighted, as had Aldrich, the interlocking nature of education and service in an urban situation. He concluded that what he called "the disease of meaninglessness" was to blame—not the crumbling of whole blocks into slums so much as "the frustration of its citizens," which allows the blocks to crumble. "No amount of bulldozing will cure that disease," he said, urging that as a first priority his hearers look for the cause of the frustration which he delineated.

He scarcely needed to suggest that lack of educational opportunities—not only for the kind of education that enables a man to better himself in his job, but for the "liberal" kind that enables him to understand a little more clearly the world he works in—is a primary cause of frustration.

Vocational education is not too hard to come by in many areas, but liberal education for adults is often much harder to find, whether for academic credit or for pure self-enlightenment. Despite the splendid efforts of a few Land-Grant universities, the burden of the findings presented by analysts at Kansas City, and other findings during the Centennial Year, is that over all they still have a long row to hoe with respect to this kind of adult education. In fact, said President John A. Perkins of the University of Delaware in his stirring keynote speech at Kansas City: "The neglect we have shown it will, if continued, be completely tragic in the future before us. . . . In our time, enlightened and devoted citizenship is *the* practical vocation of life."

CHAPTER TWO

General Extension

The instrument by which education in fields other than agriculture and home economics is brought to adults, whether it be in formal evening classes, by correspondence, or by radio or television, whether it be for credit or not, and whether it be by a Land-Grant or any other type of university, is known as "general extension."

Work in agriculture and home economics is carried on through "cooperative extension," so called because it is a joint venture of the U.S. Department of Agriculture, the Land-Grant colleges and universities, and in some cases state departments of agriculture. Cooperative extension was set up by Congress in the Smith-Lever Act of 1914. It is highly organized, with agents in every county, highly effective, in the main highly respected, and—a crucial point —well financed, by both federal and state funds.

General extension, carried on by universities alone, presents quite a different picture. There are some conspicuous exceptions—UCLA and Wisconsin were mentioned in Chapter 1, and they and some others will be examined later in this chapter—but in most states general extension falls far short of high effectiveness. It is not as a rule highly organized, it enjoys scant respect on many campuses, and —again crucially—it is usually miserably financed. Yet, because of the conditions of modern life, it is critically needed.

At Kansas City, Ralph W. Tyler, director of the Center

13

for Advanced Study in the Behavioral Sciences at Stanford, California, presented a remarkably penetrating critique of Land-Grant general extension services. In it he cited five reasons why "these services are seen as particularly crucial at this time":

1. New demands for knowledge, skills, insights and understanding growing out of the technological revolution and the international crisis.
2. The rapid accumulation of knowledge.
3. The great increase in numbers of adults seeking further education.
4. Movement of the population into urban areas.
5. Shifts in the American way of life requiring new adjustments.

With reference to the first point in particular, but with general application to all of them, it is interesting to note that the American Assembly, in a statement issued in May 1962, declared that "the readjustments demanded by technological change can more readily be comprehended and accomplished by a work force both broadly educated as citizens and highly trained as workers."

Tyler used as a take-off point a June 1961 statement by the Division of General Extension of the Land-Grant association. The statement, titled "Today's Critical Needs and University Extension," takes the position that extension should be "an intimate and essential aspect of the total enterprise of the modern public university."

The function of extension, it says, is "to identify public problems and needs, to interpret these concerns to the university, to focus university skills and resources upon them and thence to translate university insights into educational programs throughout a state or region." This, it says, "should be carried on by every available means, from resident instruction and evening classes to radio and TV, from off-campus undergraduate centers to traveling libraries and film collections, from short courses, concerts and art exhibits to formal and informal consulting services for individuals, communities, institutions, agencies and groups."

Among today's most critical needs, the statement identified the following: (1) degree work for adults whose college careers were interrupted; (2) technical, professional, and postgraduate education for persons who must keep up with developments in their field of work; (3) citizenship training for civic literacy and public responsibility; (4) opportunities for cultural, intellectual, physical, and emotional development; (5) family life, consumer education, retirement orientation; (6) urban and community development, including applied research on a wide range of urban problems; (7) labor education; (8) international education; (9) cooperation with other adult education agencies.

In sum, the position paper calls for an extension program by which "the entire university is placed in the same organic relationship to all the people of the state, *with primary emphasis on the growing urban population,* as that achieved by the Land-Grant college of agriculture with farmers."

Accepting these criteria as valid, Tyler proceeded to compare them with the existing situation as he had analyzed it from questionnaires sent to all 68 member institutions of the Land-Grant association. "The discrepancies," he observed, "are readily apparent."

To begin with, Tyler found that—although there are extenuating circumstances—"as far as the questionnaire returns show, only half the Land-Grant institutions are offering programs with some range of adult needs in mind."

The extenuating circumstances are illustrated by a fact which replies to the questionnaire did not show—that only about half, or a few over, of the Land-Grant colleges and universities are charged with responsibility for general extension by their states. There are, first, 16 predominantly Negro Land-Grant institutions which are not heavily involved in general extension. Second, there are about the same number of "separate" Land-Grant institutions in states having other state universities which took early leadership in extension. Thus, it is only the 30-odd "combined" Land-Grant institutions which are primarily involved.

Even within this fraction, however, Tyler found serious shortcomings. Perhaps as much as two-thirds of the extension resources of these institutions, he estimated, are devoted to providing opportunities on or off campus for adults whose education has been interrupted, and after that the scope of offerings is sharply constricted.

While almost all the institutions participating in general extension reported programs of continuing education at technical, professional, and postgraduate levels, the catch is that most of them are for public school teachers and administrators, who in most states get more pay if they have advanced degrees or have completed certain amounts of work toward them. A large part of the work for other groups, Tyler found, is of the "short course" variety, which he cautioned is "likely to be 'spotty' and to emphasize immediate answers to pressing problems rather than the development of broader and deeper understanding and the use of new concepts and techniques."

Here it might properly be pointed out that there is a growing trend toward *state* systems of general extension—in Florida and Oregon as two pioneering examples—under which the extension work of all state institutions of higher learning is integrated under a state board. Under such a system the role assigned to a Land-Grant university, or any single institution, might be only a part of a generally well-constructed plan. Viewed by itself, however, the Land-Grant institution might seem to be deficient.

In the remaining areas about which the Division of General Extension expressed concern—citizenship training, cultural opportunities, family life and consumer education, urban and community development, labor education, international education, and cooperation with other agencies—

Tyler found little to report. His comment regarding urban and community development might well serve as a comment on all: "This is another goal which is yet to be realized."

With regard to urban affairs it should be noted, however, that several universities carry on work in this field through channels other than extension proper. The University of Illinois, for instance, set up a Council on Community Development, the work of which is conducted by an Office of Community Development, attached to the provost's office. (The whole question of Land-Grant activity in urban affairs will be taken up in the next chapter.)

It should also be noted that in labor education, another of the areas listed by the Division of General Extension, several Land-Grant universities are gratifyingly active. Michigan State, Pennsylvania State, and Rutgers are only three that could be mentioned which have set up classes in industrial centers to bring working people not only the technical training that will help them to improve their job status but also the work in sociology, economics, the arts, which will help them to be more intelligent and thoughtful citizens.

It is fair to say, over all, that—negligent as many Land-Grant institutions may have been, and imperfectly as they may have carried out their general extension mission—they have done better than most other universities, public or private.

Nevertheless, in light of their tradition of reaching out to the people, the Land-Grant universities have failed so far to measure up as Tyler and the Division of General Extension think they should. Why?

It has been mentioned that, in contrast to cooperative extension, general extension is very poorly financed. For the most part, in the words of President Herbert Albrecht of North Dakota State University, "it is operated on a ticket-selling basis." That is, it is largely paid for directly by the persons participating in the short courses, summer session, or whatever. Since the services of cooperative extension are generally provided free, or virtually so—and people know it—it often is difficult to make a case for charging for general extension.

Half of the Land-Grant universities reporting to Tyler said that general extension receives less than 25 per cent of its support from state sources. About half said that extension's administrative costs were supported with university funds but that all other costs had to be met from income. Among other university presidents, Albrecht believes that "general extension is a perfectly legitimate activity for state—or federal—government to support."

Proposals for the federal support of general extension have been introduced in Congress off and on for years, with the support of both the Association of State Universities and Land-Grant Colleges and of the State Universities Association, the latter representing those state universities which are not Land-Grant. The point of view of these two associations, as stated at a Senate Education Subcommittee hearing by John T. Caldwell, chancellor of North Carolina State College and 1962 president of the Land-Grant association, is this:

> This generation of Americans faces responsibilities of appalling complexity in adjusting its politics and institutions to the foreign and domestic imperatives of our times. The discharge of these responsibilities, depending as it does on the personal, social and political effectiveness of the average American citizen, demands increased efforts in adult education.
>
> Given adequate financial resources . . . our extension divisions can lead the way in a most rewarding kind of education: that of teaching people how to do their jobs better and how to lead richer lives. The purpose of education is, after all, not to earn grades and credits, but to improve judgment and to advance knowledge. The more the universities can relate academic studies to the solution of actual problems of urban life and work, the more effective education will become.

Next to financing, Tyler's questionnaires showed, the most difficult problem is the fact that "there is no long tradition of the extension teacher," and next to that the related problem of "achieving recognition and full status for extension as an educational division of the university."

The lack of an extension teaching tradition means that it is difficult to recruit people to do this kind of work and even more difficult to persuade resident faculty to participate in it. The consequences of lack of status for extension are many. The faculty often will not recognize extension credits as equivalent to residence credits, for one thing, and, for another, extension staff members seldom have the same opportunity for advancement as resident faculty or hold faculty rank.

"A common view," Tyler summarized, "seems to be that extension services are good things to provide if they can be made available largely on a self-supporting basis and if they do not require much time from the major faculty members."

The underlying problem is the long-standing academic view that the university's primary responsibilities are research and resident teaching and that anything else is of marginal importance. This attitude often extends to the extension director himself, who may well have had the assignment "wished off on him."

"The cross that general extension has to bear, aside from finances," Albrecht said, "is the collection of faint hearts who are responsible for it. At a recent conference on continuing education which I attended one fellow said he wanted to keep on teaching one resident course so that he could 'retain his academic status.' If people feel that way about it, they'd better get out."

For all the documented faults of the many universities with respect to general extension, much good work is being done by the few, and numerous others are undertaking serious self-examinations, seeking ways to make their extension efforts more effective. While circumstances obviously vary from state to state, a glance at a few institutions which are generally recognized as doing good work should provide some worthwhile ideas for the residents of states who are interested in promoting adult education work by their own universities.

The Los Angeles campus of the University of California and the University of Wisconsin have already been mentioned. At UCLA some 10,000 adults are enrolled in evening classes ranging from liberal arts work taken for simple personal satisfaction to highly technical study by engineers employed by the massive spacecraft industry of the area.

Such a program as UCLA's is, of course, feasible only in a large metropolitan area and possible only when it has the full backing which such an institution as the University of California is committed to give. On and through all the seven campuses and one extension center which it had in 1962 (the Irvine campus was still on the drafting board), California enrolled 150,000 extension students, making it by far the biggest adult education operation in any U.S. university.

Where there is no such concentration of people as in Los Angeles, other means can be effectively used. The University of Wisconsin, whose motto is "The boundaries of the campus are the boundaries of the state," began in 1906 to take education to the people. Today, in addition to its full-university-status Milwaukee branch, it operates eight undergraduate campuses at strategic locations around the state, all of which double as adult education centers, with faculty from all divisions of the central campus at Madison teaching several nights a week.

In Indiana, Purdue operates an extensive system of centers similar to those in Wisconsin. The Ohio State University has been rapidly developing a chain of two-year branches, including a major one at Wright-Patterson Air Force Base near Dayton, and another one for Dayton generally in cooperation with Miami University, which also is a state institution.

The University of Delaware, which conducts extension work on its campus at Newark, also has centers at Dover and Wilmington. It has almost as many extension students as it has regular undergraduates.

The University of Maryland, which conducts an elaborate extension program for the Washington, D.C., area as well as statewide, operates another extension activity which is unique among all universities. This is its overseas program, undertaken at the request of the U.S. government, for the benefit of Americans stationed overseas.

In 1962 these were located in 25 countries: Ethiopia, the Azores, Bermuda, France, Germany, Greece, Greenland, Guam, Iceland, Italy, Japan, Korea, Labrador, Libya, Morocco, Newfoundland, Norway, Okinawa, Pakistan, Saudi Arabia, Spain, Taiwan, the Netherlands, Turkey, and the United Kingdom.

Pennsylvania State University in 1962 undertook a plan to expand the capacity of its statewide chain of undergraduate campuses and technical institutes so that by 1970 an opportunity for at least two years of higher education will be within commuting distance of an estimated 97 per cent of the state's population.

In some other states, Land-Grant and other state universities have found that their means or the scattered nature of their states' populations makes establishment of a system of adult instructional centers impractical, at least for the present. Instead they have concentrated on correspondence work or have set up "continuing education centers" on their campuses where short courses, conferences, and the like are held.

The pioneer center of this sort was set up by Minnesota in the 1920's. Michigan State, Georgia, and Nebraska, which was also an early leader in correspondence work, are among institutions which have started them in more recent years. The University of Missouri designated as an educational center a 13-story building in St. Louis which it received by bequest in 1961.

Obviously, though, no number of off-campus or on-campus centers is going to make the difference if there is no real commitment to extension on the part of the faculty, and no real concept of university commitment on the part of the administration. The point here is well illustrated by the way in which the Land-Grant Michigan State University conducts its general extension program in contrast to the procedure at another large institution in another state.

At Michigan State, every college has an assistant dean for continuing education. These assistants meet regularly with their deans and with the department heads of their colleges and are very much members of the policy-making body of the colleges. Faculty members, too, are fully involved and spend a significant part of their time on extension work.

At the other institution in question, also Land-Grant, the setup looks very much the same—on paper. But here the faculty has hardly heard of it. "We believe in adult education," the dean of arts and science told a recent visitor, "but I don't permit our faculty to do it except on campus." At this university extension instructors are drawn from the faculties of the four-year colleges which dot the state and are hired part-time by the university.

In no field is adult education in a more precarious position than in arts and science. With a few notable exceptions, the Land-Grant and other state universities have had little luck in enlisting the support of historians, artists, "pure" scientists, and other members of their faculties of arts and science in contributing their talents and knowledge to a nonresident clientele.

Seth Russell, the thoughtful dean of arts and science at North Dakota State University, took leave during the spring semester of 1961 to make a study of "A & S" extension work at state universities, Land-Grant and non-Land-Grant. The study was made for the Center for the Study of Liberal Education for Adults, which is located in Chicago and is financed by the Ford Foundation's Fund for Adult Education.

On his return Russell cited what he called the "archtypical approach" to extension, expressed by the arts and science dean of a plains state Land-Grant university: "How can we justify taking a man out of a laboratory and sending him down to Podunk to teach an evening class? How can we justify bringing a man back too tired to teach his regular classes? With the money we have, don't we have to spend our time with young people?"

Thus far, this dean might be regarded as simply the victim of circumstances, willing to do more if he could. But then, Russell added, he tipped his hand by continuing: "Anyway, our job is to train the elite."

In contrast, Russell recalled the comment of William Bevan, the new dean of arts and science at the Land-Grant Kansas State University: "We are spending too much on undergraduates who shouldn't be in college. Why not share our resources with their parents, who have better motivation?"

To which Russell himself added: "If the humanities, the new mathematics, the new sociology are good and valid, they don't belong exclusively to the adolescent. Everybody is entitled to share in them."

Inevitably in any discussion of how to extend extension, the suggestion comes up of combining general with cooperative extension. Attractive and practical as this idea may appear at first blush, many people in both kinds of extension are uneasy about it. As Tyler said at Kansas City, "there are several unique elements in the early development of cooperative extension which would not apply to other groups."

Tyler's view was bolstered by that of Earl Coke, a former U.S. assistant secretary of agriculture and now a vice president of the Bank of America, who at Kansas City evaluated Land-Grant work in agriculture.

While he conceded that "few other parts of the Land-Grant universities are as experienced in the college-to-people approach" as the agricultural colleges, Coke took issue with a 1958 report by the Federal Extension Service which proposed that cooperative extension broaden its activities to include such things as "family living," "community improvement," and "public affairs."

"To the degree that the adult educational effort (of cooperative extension) moves into areas other than commercial agriculture," he declared, "it approaches the purposes and audience of general extension."

Coke did not commit himself against merger, but he did caution that any such step "not be abrupt, that there be a period of cooperation and coordination to allow time for experience to dictate the best form of organization and activity."

Actually, even before Coke spoke, two Land-Grant institutions, the University of Missouri and Utah State University, had combined their two services into one university extension division. In most cases, the former county agents of Missouri's cooperative extension service remain, but they are now known as university extension agents, coordinating all types of adult education programs. It is planned to rotate a few of these men into Columbia from time to time for work leading to an M.A. degree. The project, all concerned agree, is too young to conclude whether it will succeed or fail, but it is being watched with decided interest.

The Missouri and Utah State plans and similar schemes obviously anticipate a willingness by cooperative and general extension to get together on some basis. Where this is plainly never going to happen, but where there is some degree of will to develop general extension in the arts and sciences, an experiment now under way at a non-Land-Grant state university may offer a solution in some cases.

The University of Oklahoma, with assistance from the Fund for Adult Education, is trying out a program leading to a degree called Bachelor of Liberal Studies. Thirty selected students—ranch wives, small businessmen, a cross section of the state's non-college-graduate population, aged on the average about 40 years—are receiving three-year scholarships which enable them to participate in the experiment.

The first step is for the students to spend a week at the Norman campus, taking many tests and spending considerable time with people on the humanities, natural science, and social science faculties. At the end of this time they decide on one of these three fields in which to do their first year's work. Then they go home and read in this field for a year.

At the end of the year they come back to Norman for three weeks of intensive work, culminating in a comprehensive examination. They then repeat the same procedure in the other two fields. The hope, of course, is that close campus contacts by students will remove many faculty doubts about the worth of extension.

Oklahoma is what is called a "separate" state university, as are universities in other states where there is a state-supported institution in addition to the Land-Grant university which all 50 states have. By and large, despite such evidences of willingness as that displayed at Oklahoma, the separate universities have not been out in front in their adult education efforts any more than have the majority of Land-Grant institutions.

Although Land-Grant efforts are still admittedly feeble in many areas, the truth of a statement in a recent report by Cyril Houle, professor of education at the University of Chicago, is challengingly evident. In a pamphlet written for the Center for the Study of Liberal Education for Adults, called "Major Trends in Higher Adult Education," Houle contended: "The whole course of higher adult education, in all its aspects, will be influenced by the events which take place on Land-Grant college campuses in the next few years."

CHAPTER THREE

Community Affairs

Growing need for strictly educational activities among the people of their states has in no way diminished the Land-Grant institutions' historic obligation of *service* to these same people through the practical application of knowledge.

In recent years, and most especially since World War II, the most spectacular need for increased services has been to cities. Beset by overcrowding and all its attendant afflictions, jammed transportation, decaying neighborhoods, overburdened schools and the like, the cities need the kind of attention that a university's roster of sociologists, economists, and other professional people can supply.

Yet the problem of the cities, it is now becoming recognized, is only part of a much bigger problem. The pronounced migration of rural and small-town people into the cities, because it *is* the most spectacular element, has received the most general attention. What has not been so generally appreciated is that these people leave some very serious problems behind in the areas where they came from—and that these problems are sometimes aggravated by city people moving to the country.

As seen now, the broad problem involves three principal elements: (1) the central city; (2) the suburbs; (3) the "fringe area" beyond the suburbs. The remaining strictly rural areas, to be sure, still have their own problems, but

26

rural problems will be treated in the later chapter on agriculture.

The three areas now to be considered admittedly overlap, sometimes so perplexingly in fact that, rather than some such term as "urban affairs" or "urban renewal," the designation "community affairs" seems to describe more accurately the questions that must be taken up in connection with them.

Land-Grant institutions, particularly those located in states with large metropolitan complexes, are well aware of this, as is dramatically spotlighted by the way the Ford Foundation has distributed grants under its Urban and Regional Program.

In its 1961 annual report, the Foundation noted especially that "several Land-Grant institutions, established when 85 per cent of the population lived in rural areas, are starting their second century by turning their services to a society that is now 70 per cent urbanized." Among some 60 universities, associations, and other groups interested in community affairs which had benefited under this program since 1955, Land-Grant institutions were among those receiving the largest amounts—Wisconsin, $1,035,000; Rutgers, the state university of New Jersey, $950,000; Delaware, $500,000; Illinois, $125,000; and Purdue, $100,000.

Other Land-Grant universities received Ford grants for more specialized studies in this general field. They include Pennsylvania State, which participates in the work of the Allegheny Council to Improve Our Neighborhoods (Pittsburgh), California, Missouri, Minnesota, and the Massachusetts Institute of Technology. The Ford-financed projects, of course, are quite aside from what the named universities and other Land-Grant institutions are doing under other auspices or out of their own funds.

Although work in community affairs among other universities is considerable in some cases, this chapter will concentrate on the projects at Purdue, Rutgers, Delaware, and Wisconsin as illustrative of work in each of the three general types of communities—Purdue and Rutgers in a central city, Delaware in an urban-suburban area, and Wisconsin in a fringe area.

Purdue got into urban redevelopment in the early 1950's, when civic and industrial leaders in East Chicago, in the heart of northern Indiana's Calumet industrial complex, asked for help in arresting the blight that was engulfing the city's small residential area.

As a result of the appeal by civic leaders, the university's Division of Educational Reference conducted a housing survey, paid for by two of East Chicago's steel companies. Fifty graduate students canvassed a sampling of families and discovered that 47 per cent wanted to move. At about the same time the city of East Chicago made a study which demonstrated need for an early and drastic attack on violations of fire, health, and building codes.

The problem of East Chicago is intensified by the fact that nearly 90 per cent of its 7,402 acres are devoted to industry, with its 57,000 residents crammed into less than 1,000 acres. Since it is entirely surrounded by other similarly compacted cities on three sides, and by Lake Michigan on the fourth, there is no room to expand the residential area. New housing, therefore, had to be created by eradicating slums.

To move on the problem, Purdue recommended the establishment of a foundation as a rallying point. In 1954 the Purdue-Calumet Development Foundation was incorporated with these objectives: to establish comprehensive city plans, to obtain revision of city ordinances where indicated, to eliminate slums and blight and to improve and enlarge the housing supply, to improve the general environment of the city, and—very important—to develop public understanding and support of these goals.

By 1962 the PCDF, the city's own Redevelopment Commission, and other groups had acquired 268 parcels of property and were helping to relocate 600 families and 32 businesses, with the ultimate goal of relocating 2,000 families.

Among other accomplishments, 80 acres of a new residential subdivision, Prairie Park Development, had been built on land acquired from a steel company, with 189 acres eventually to be occupied. An 86-family apartment building had been opened, peopled largely by former residents of a condemned 367-acre area of slums. The city's entire sewer system had been renovated, parks improved, and several new municipal buildings completed.

A Family Service Program, sponsored jointly by PCDF and the university's nearby Calumet branch campus, offers displaced families help in adjusting to new situations and in finding new homes. It was to help train social workers for this phase of the project that the Ford Foundation made its $100,000 grant.

Eventually, says Dean C. H. Lawshe of the University Extension Administration, the Calumet campus may train "a unique type of extension worker," applying techniques of agricultural extension to urban problems. Already a group of Purdue agricultural extension people have toured Lake County, in which the Calumet industrial area is located, to study the possibilities.

Eventually, too, he hopes that the Calumet area can become a sort of university laboratory for scholars in the behavioral sciences, engineering, and other fields connected with urban problems.

A project similar to Purdue's, but on a rather larger scale, and with several additional elements involved, got under way in New Jersey in an exploratory way in 1962, financed by the Ford grant to Rutgers.

The opportunity, and need, for Rutgers to emphasize urban affairs was obvious. New Jersey, forty-sixth in area among the 50 states, is the most urbanized state in the union. More than five million of its slightly over six million residents live in communities of 2,500 or more, including Newark, with more than 400,000; Jersey City, with more than 275,000; and Paterson, with nearly 150,000.

The Rutgers project is being managed by its Urban Studies Center, which has its own full-time staff, headed by

John E. Bebout, a New Jersey native and graduate of Rutgers who for 14 years was assistant director of the National Municipal League. The Center was decided upon as a device through which the resources of all departments of the university could be most effectively channeled.

In December 1961 Harry C. Bredemeier of the Center proposed "an action research program to expand the opportunities of underprivileged youth in a slum area and to improve youth's incentives to take advantage of such expanded opportunities." As a consequence, President Gross appointed a Committee on Human Aspects of Urban Renewal, with Bredemeier as chairman and including a representative from each of the following divisions of the university: the Graduate School of Education, the Graduate School of Social Work, the School of Business, the Institute of Management and Labor Relations, the Law School, the School of Library Studies, the Eagleton Institute of Politics, the College of Nursing, and the departments of history, economics, psychology, political science, and sociology. Each divisional representative became chairman of a subcommittee in his division.

In May 1962, after conferences with the mayor and other officials of the city of Newark, all of whom responded enthusiastically, a slum area within that city was selected as the "target" for the project. That very summer the Research Division of the Center set to work to gather basic data from census materials and school records, preparatory to research on the values and attitudes of young people in the target area, their reading habits, job aspirations, and family patterns.

In the fall, various subcommittees wheeled into action also. For example, the Social Work Subcommittee began making arrangements with the Newark Council of Social Agencies, the United Fund, the Jewish Welfare Board, and various Catholic welfare agencies to coordinate and extend services to the families of "troubled" students. Arrangements also were begun to work with such public agencies as probation, parole, welfare, employment, housing, health, and police.

Concurrently with this, and later as necessary basic data became available, other subcommittees began working with appropriate agencies in Newark, all looking toward a beginning of actual work with youth in the fall of 1963.

One thing Bredemeier emphasized from the start: "The university must not attempt to become a substitute local government, school board or welfare agency by actually carrying out the opportunity-enhancing enterprises we have been considering. Rather, the university should stimulate and help local agencies to carry them out."

The project is, under these terms, essentially an educational extension project in which knowledge available to and newly gathered by the university is brought to the people, in this case such people as the heads of welfare agencies and health departments, who can put this knowledge to work in the best Land-Grant tradition. Ultimately Rutgers hopes to broaden its urban work to take in, first, one or more of the "inner ring" of older Newark suburbs and then an "outer ring" area. Ultimately, too, it hopes to do some work in a fringe area.

Another important aspect of the Rutgers project is a three-year experimental program of fellowships for study of urban problems, awarded to five candidates each year from such fields as journalism, government, business, and voluntary service organizations. Financed by $200,000 of the Ford grant, the program began in the fall of 1961. Its fourfold purpose is: (1) to improve effectiveness of the fellows when they return to their jobs; (2) to deepen the university's understanding of the difficulties under which these people sometimes have to work; (3) to get their ideas on how the university might work more effectively with urban agencies; (4) to encourage the fellows to expand their responsibilities as citizens in a nonoccupational way.

Delaware, New Jersey's neighbor to the south, offers opportunity to examine a somewhat different type of program. Delaware is even smaller in area than New Jersey, but it is somewhat less widely urbanized. It does have 10 cities of over 2,500 population—but, with two exceptions, not much over. The exceptions are Newark, which is the seat of the state university and which has about 12,000 inhabitants, and the state's only real metropolis, Wilmington, with 95,000. Both these places, and most of the other larger communities, are located in New Castle County, the smallest in area of the state's three counties, occupying less than one-fourth of the total area, at the northern end of the state.

The university set up a Division of Urban Affairs in 1961, upon receiving its Ford grant. In its proposal to the foundation it had stated the aims and goals of the division in this way:

The primary purpose would be to develop . . . a program of extension, research and education. This program is designed to translate and expand the Land-Grant college approach so successful in the rural field to the urban setting which predominates in our state and times.

This program would be developed over a five-year period. It would directly involve appropriate schools, divisions and departments of the university; it would seek to involve citizens and organizations in a wide variety of ways; it would provide assistance and stimulation to public officials and governments, and it would utilize all the communities of the state as classrooms in which to learn about and help meet problems of urbanization.

As its first project the Division undertook to collaborate with the Greater Wilmington Development Council in an effort to establish a planning process for New Castle County, which presents the usual pattern of the metropolitan area. Wilmington, the central city, has been declining in population, with the county area outside Wilmington characterized by "urban sprawl." After exhaustive preliminary studies, the Division early in 1962 invited state, county, and city officials to a luncheon meeting to discuss the possibility of creating formal regional planning machinery. As the outcome of this meeting, two committees were set up. One was composed of public officials and was designated the Joint Regional Planning Policy Committee. The other, made up of professional planners and engineers, was called the Technical Advisory Committee on Regional Planning.

One of the first concrete steps toward planning was to enlist the aid of the governor in an effort to include New Castle County in the area served by the Penn-Jersey Transportation Study, a logical procedure since the county is linked to both states by the Delaware River bridge and the New Jersey Turnpike. Contact with the governor was made by the Policy Committee. The Advisory Committee, meanwhile, began work on a design for a regional planning program which was to provide importantly for cooperation among various planning agencies and officials working in the county.

"An overriding consideration," the Division's first annual report emphasized, in words reminiscent of Bredemeier's in New Jersey, "is the importance of creating organizational arrangements and a climate of opinion among public officials that will lead to substantial implementation of any plans that are formulated."

In the early stages of the Delaware project, the final role of the Division—what it might do once a planning program for New Castle County was agreed upon—was uncertain. It was considered likely that it would at least enter into contracts to do parts of the planning research. Or, in its status as a neutral among the various jurisdictions involved, it was considered as a possible agency to administer the entire program.

One thing that did happen almost immediately was that the city of Newark contracted with the Division to prepare, over a two-year term, a comprehensive plan for the city within the forthcoming county plan and, in effect, to continue after that as a permanent city planning staff. The Division was not eager, however, to plunge into too much active planning until it knew just where it was going.

Consequently, another thing that was done early in the game was to compile an inventory of 297 surveys and reports that had already been made in the Wilmington area.

While the University of Delaware began its community affairs project in the Wilmington–New Castle County area —mainly because the problems were already posed and because the climate was right—it is by no means forgetting the rest of the state.

"Except for the state government, New Castle County, and the city of Wilmington," the Division's report pointed out, "all of the other units of government in Delaware are probably too small to justify a full-time professional planning staff. The Division of Urban Affairs will maintain a small group of planners to render continuing planning assistance and prepare comprehensive or master plans for the smaller units of government. . . . If the down-state municipalities can be stimulated to embrace effective planning programs, they should have one of the most useful tools yet devised to meet the expected rapid urbanization."

In pursuit of this phase of the plan, shortly after signing of the Newark contract, Division Director Edward S. Overman announced a four-phase program providing first for missionary efforts among local officials, followed by signing of a contract when a community is ready for one, with basic research and liaison work among county, city, and state officials to be carried on continually. A key man will be an "urban agent" who will travel around the state working on much the same basis as agricultural county agents have worked for two generations. "It may take three years to find out if it will work," Overman conceded, "but we feel that, as a university agency, we have a responsibility to experiment."

The third type of area in which Land-Grant universities are at work in community affairs is what sociologists describe as the "fringe area." Just what a fringe area is has never been defined too precisely, except that it differs from a suburb in that the latter generally includes no farms.

Where suburb ends and fringe begins is often difficult to determine. Even more difficult to determine is where fringe ends and genuine rural area begins.

The question was taken up at some length by several speakers from Land-Grant institutions at the 1962 meeting of the American Country Life Association in Washington, D.C. Glenn V. Fuguitt of Wisconsin suggested a working definition of "fringe area" as "a zone in transition . . . moving from rural to urban in land use, occupational structure and social organization. What is fringe today is city or suburb tomorrow."

An area of this sort is populated by, or is at least coming to be populated by, people classified by the U.S. Census as "rural non-farm." These would include commuters, both former city dwellers who keep their city jobs and people who have left the farm to work in the city, but it may also include many onetime farmers who continue to live in the fringe area and to work there in off-farm employment, in a cannery or feed mill perhaps, or as service workers.

In any case, it was noted by Mervin G. Smith and John B. Mitchell of The Ohio State University in a paper read before the Association: "Conditions for conflict between newcomers and old-time residents are excellent in this no man's land between farm and city. . . . The ex-urbanite wishes to add conveniences, facilities and services he has grown accustomed to in the city. These changes entail more taxes, levies, or bond issues. The older resident has always regarded the area as 'a good place to live, and why change it?'" Adding to the problems of the fringe area, among many other things, is the fact that existing township, village, or other governmental structures often cannot cope with modern demands.

The way to orderly conversion of a fringe to a suburban or even urban area obviously is not easy—"even if," as Selz C. Mayo of the Land-Grant North Carolina State College told the Country Life group, "we knew all the components" of the problem. Nevertheless, Mayo said, certain guidelines are apparent. The first of these, he continued, "is the fuller use of existing resources" by leaders in the area, and prominently among these "are the total resources of the Land-Grant college, including the Agricultural Extension Service and the engineering extension division."

A rather clear-cut example of a fringe area, its problems and an effort to solve them, is offered by the project being carried on by the University of Wisconsin in its Columbia County Demonstration Area.

Like Rutgers, Delaware, and other universities, Wisconsin concerns itself in urban and suburban areas as well as in the fringe area. It has a major project in Milwaukee and one in the Fox River Valley, a two-county area fairly well filled with such medium-sized cities as Oshkosh, Appleton, and Kaukauna. And, as is well known, its cooperative extension work in rural areas is among the best in the nation. The Columbia County project, however, as stated before, offers a rather clear-cut example of work in a fringe area.

Columbia County is just to the north of Dane County, where Madison, the county seat and also the state capital and the seat of the university, is located. It embraces 778 square miles and some 37,000 inhabitants. The county seat and principal city of Columbia County is Portage, with about 8,000 population.

What makes it particularly appropriate for a fringe area study is its proximity to Dane County and Madison. A Madison fringe area in Dane County, delineated as recently as 1946, has long since been incorporated into the city or its suburban villages. Columbia County, with nearly 27,000 of its 37,000 population designated as non-farm in the 1960 census, has only about 3,000 of its 13,000 employed persons working in agriculture. Part of it, at least, will plainly be affected by Madison's further expansion.

The project got under way in January 1961 with appointment of a committee to develop criteria for the area to be studied and to recommend an area matching them as nearly as possible. The committee also was to recommend a pattern of operation. Some of the criteria decided upon were: the area should be predominantly rural, have a net out-migration of population, have a varied pattern of social and economic problems in both agricultural and nonagricultural segments of the population, be within 100 miles of Madison, and have a county board of supervisors and cooperative extension personnel with a special interest in the project.

With Columbia County identified as most nearly filling the bill, the next step was to bolster the four-member cooperative extension staff at Portage with two more persons, their salaries and expenses to be shared by the Ford Foundation and the county and cooperative extension funds.

This team set to work to identify, with help from local people and the university staff, the problems and interests of Columbia County, both rural and urban, agricultural and nonagricultural. The next step was to develop an action program involving specialists from whatever university departments might be of assistance.

Although the cooperative extension service is responsible for administering the project, much of the program will be educational, and may involve credit and noncredit courses, workshops, meetings with groups, and individual counseling with county officials and nongovernmental leaders. This part of the work will be under Professor Paul J. Grogan, chairman of engineering extension at the university, who was named as coordinator of all three Wisconsin community affairs projects—Milwaukee, Fox Valley, and Columbia County. A key part of the whole enterprise is the naming of countywide study and planning groups of citizens to give advisory direction.

Manifestly, the greater part of what has been done under any of the programs sketched in this chapter falls in the realm of research and tooling-up. The whole problem descended upon the universities so suddenly during a period when they were heavily preoccupied with the simple difficulty of handling swollen on-campus enrollments, that little more could have been done earlier. The significant point is that the Land-Grant universities have recognized that their mandate of service extends to people swept up by the wave of urbanization and all the implications of it.

What these implications are was expressed by Mayor Arthur Naftalin of Minneapolis, an alumnus of the University of Minnesota and a former professor of political science there, in remarks prepared for the Kansas City Convocation: "It is the function of higher education to help the community to understand the nature of its future. Now more than ever it serves as the main source of enlarged insight into social process, of generating guide lines for humane and democratic action, of providing greater public enlightenment and more knowledge concerning man's problems. Now more than ever higher education must assist the community in becoming the master of its own future."

CHAPTER FOUR

International Affairs

We as a nation are now in the world for keeps; our involvement in world affairs is not just a passing phase of our national life; our survival depends upon the creation of mutually beneficial relations with other nations.

This demands growth in our world view. It needs a design big enough to include all mankind. It requires that each individual include the whole world in his circle of concern; that American interests become more closely identified in the minds of people throughout the world with human interests.

The forces of education have a responsibility to prepare the citizens for intelligent, effective participation in today's world. This responsibility we have not yet taken with the seriousness it deserves.

With these challenging words, after months of patient research and exchange of ideas, International Study Group III began its report at the Kansas City Convocation.

There were four study groups in all, each examining different aspects of the vast pattern of international activity into which American colleges and universities are weaving themselves, with particular attention to how the Land-Grant institutions are fulfilling their part of the total obligation. The study groups, and the assigned topic of each, were:

I. *The special role of Land-Grant colleges and state universities in meeting the needs of developing nations* (chairman, Professor H. W. Hannah of Illinois).

II. *Steps needed to improve or develop programs to meet*

the needs of foreign scholars, students, and trainees (chairman, Dean John McConnell of Cornell).

III. *Education of Americans to serve abroad—and of America to an understanding of this country's role in world affairs* (chairman, Professor Harvey Baty of Montana State College).

IV. *How far should government—state and federal—go toward support of public higher education in international programs?* (chairman, Vice President Harry R. Wellman of California).

As often happens, topics set up in advance do not prove to be so handy as it had been supposed they would be. In this case, as the studies turned out in the end, the second part of Group III's report and the generalized, philosophical portions of Group IV's fell logically together. This chapter will concentrate on those portions of these two reports. The succeeding three chapters will take up in order the findings of Groups I and II and the first part of the report of Group III. The particularized findings of Group IV, which explore the extent to which state and federal governments should support specific kinds of programs, will be brought to bear in these chapters at appropriate places.

Each committee submitted recommendations in its own area, but when all reports were in the chairmen decided to consolidate them. The consolidated recommendations appear separately as Chapter 8.

Group III lost little time, as it continued its report, in applying itself to the Land-Grant aspects of international affairs:

"Education applied to the needs of life" has been a distinctive contribution of the Land-Grant colleges in the past 100 years. This concept is being increasingly accepted by all education. The time has come for the Land-Grant colleges to work with all forces of education to build a world in which all human beings can survive and thrive.

The Land-Grant colleges, by their philosophy, experience, and organization, are uniquely equipped to assist in this task. Many of them have already assumed such responsibilities. This is shown by the fact that . . . Land-Grant colleges and universities have 26 per cent of the foreign students, 36 per cent of the foreign faculty in the United States, 41 per cent of the U.S. faculty serving abroad, 46 per cent of ICA-financed [1] college contracts abroad, and 70 per cent of ICA college contract funds.

In addition, in the Land-Grant colleges and universities there are some 15,000 faculty members in the Extension Service. These constitute tremendous resources for education at the grass roots or community level.

But, the report continued, "even with all these resources, serious questions remain. Are all the Land-Grant colleges ready to build an international dimension into their education? Is the Extension Service willing to accept 'education in world affairs' as a part of its responsibility? Do we have personnel with the philosophy to support such education? Will the citizens, who support our institutions, consider this a legitimate undertaking for the colleges?"

The last question, of course, is intimately involved with the problem to which Group IV addressed itself. How far government *should* go in supporting programs of international education is perhaps academic. As a practical political matter, it might better be asked how far government *can* go in view of prevailing public sentiment.

As if to underline this consideration, Group III observed: "Education of America to an understanding of this country's role in world affairs is a great task. It is difficult in part because there is no clear national consensus about 'world affairs' or the role educational institutions should play in world affairs education. Many segments of our population do not consider 'international understanding' a desirable focus for public education or private thinking. In some circles, 'international' is a synonym for 'un-American.'"

Nevertheless, Baty and his colleagues found, "some Land-Grant colleges and state universities are finding a

[1] Since the report was written, the U.S. government's International Cooperation Administration (ICA) has been superseded by the Agency for International Development (AID).

way to give emphasis to world affairs education." They cited programs at Kansas State University and Michigan State University as distinctive.

Kansas State, of which Group III member James A. Mc-Cain is president, is deeply involved in international activities, with the vigorous support of its board of regents, the state legislature, and people throughout the state. These programs come under the following categories: (1) an India contract program, financed by AID, under which the university is participating in plans to improve agricultural colleges and to promote the country's growth and development, the results of which may be observed in the expansion and advancement of Indian agricultural colleges and in their development as centers for teaching, research, and extension; (2) participation in the International Farm Youth Exchange Program, through the university's extension service, which involves more farm youths than similar programs in any other state; (3) affiliation, under State Department auspices, with the Justus Liebig University in Giessen, Germany; (4) an on-campus foreign student program in which approximately 400 students from foreign countries were enrolled in 1961-62; (5) short-term training programs conducted for official foreign visitors, Eisenhower International Exchange Fellows, and AID participants.

"These programs," the group reported,

are understood, appreciated, and generously supported by the citizens of the state. One evidence of such support is the recent action of their Board of Regents. When they increased non-resident tuition, they simultaneously waived non-resident tuition for students from foreign countries, thus making them honorary "citizens" of Kansas during their university years. . . .Service clubs have provided financial assistance for foreign students. Hundreds of Kansas families have been host to foreign students during holidays, the number of invitations exceeding the number of foreign students.

McCain lists these reasons for this widespread interest and support: (1) Many people of Kansas have been participating in United Nations and world affairs activities for many years. (2) International programs and activities have received enlightened coverage in the press. (3) Foreign students, through their visits and talks throughout the state, have helped to build this favorable attitude. (4) University publications about international programs have been sent to newspapers, radio and TV stations, legislators, regents, university alumni, and many other influential persons.

Points 3 and 4, obviously, reflect an aggressive attitude by the university, of a sort which Group III felt could be well emulated.

Michigan State, after many years of increasing interest and involvement in international education, appointed the first dean of international programs in 1956. His functions were defined broadly to include not only administrative responsibilities but developmental activities related to the role of the university in the international field.

In January 1957 the various overseas projects of the university were made the administrative responsibility of the dean of international programs. Each project continues to be tied closely to relevant colleges for subject-matter guidance and support, with the exact arrangement varying from one project to another depending on the fields covered and the scope of the project.

The overseas projects include: (1) work with the National University of Colombia in the development of two agricultural colleges, with support from AID, the National University of Colombia, and the Kellogg Foundation; (2) education in business administration at Brazilian universities, a project backed by the Brazilian government and the School of Business Administration of Sao Paulo; (3) two village aid programs in Pakistan in cooperation with the Ford Foundation and the government of Pakistan; (4) establishment of a new University of Nsukka, Nigeria, with support by AID and the Inter-University Council of Great Britain.

Faculty seminars were organized in 1958 and 1959 to think through the university's objectives in the international sphere. These faculty groups, aided by Ford Foundation funds, were organized in five functional areas—politics and administration, economics and business, education, communications, and cross-cultural exchange.

Broadly stated, the aims which they established for the international program can be summarized as follows:

1. *Education of an enlightened citizenry.* To produce graduates who are capable of understanding, evaluating, and actively participating in international affairs. Regardless of the major study field of the student, it is assumed that he should leave the university able to assume the role of an enlightened citizen in matters related to international affairs.

2. *Expansion of knowledge.* To expand existing knowledge about international and cross-cultural affairs through faculty research and student interest.

3. *Training of specialists.* To help develop university programs which will produce technical specialists able to use their abilities in foreign settings in a productive and adaptable manner.

4. *Improvement of technical cooperation.* To continue to extend the technical knowledge and capabilities of the university to less developed areas in a constantly improving manner.

At Michigan State University the general education social science course, a three-quarter program which enrolls *all* entering students at the university, is being revised to include more international materials. Significant also is the fact that the office of the dean of international programs is financed by the normal budget of the university from state funds. Special activities such as overseas projects, research, international travel, are supported by contract funds or foundation grants.

Further tangible evidence that Michigan State takes seriously its commitment to international education was a week-long Conference on Educational Institutions and International Labor on its campus in March 1962.

The conference was sponsored jointly by the MSU Labor and Industrial Relations Center, the MSU Office of International Programs, AID, and the Land-Grant Centennial Office, and brought together labor union leaders, government officials, and educators from virtually all parts of the free world—from Colombia, from Nigeria, and from Turkey, India, Malaya, and Finland, to name only a few countries.

A similar tangible demonstration of commitment came later in the spring of 1962, when The Ohio State University sponsored—as a contribution to the Land-Grant Centennial observance, as was the MSU conference—a three-day symposium on "The Role of Food in World Peace," which explored in particular the responsibilities of Land-Grant institutions in agriculture and agricultural education overseas.

Despite these and other evidences elsewhere of real involvement in international affairs, however, Group III concluded that there still is a widespread lack of agreement among educators regarding this area of endeavor.

"There is no clear consensus," it said, "about the extent to which a university should become involved officially. There are some educators who insist that the responsibility of the university should be limited to the campus and those who come to it. To provide world affairs education for these, if done adequately, would be a significant achievement. Others would like to place no limits to the range of the university participation except those of interest and capability."

For its own part, Group III suggested this guideline: "It is not the responsibility of the forces of education to make foreign policy, but it is their responsibility to create an informed citizenry."

Conceding that "few universities can do everything which is desirable in world affairs education," it nevertheless listed some things which in its opinion "every college or university could do."

As on-campus activities it proposed that colleges (1) provide hospitality for foreign students and make effective use of their presence on the campus; (2) build an international dimension into courses in the social sciences; (3) encourage student participation in voluntary activities related to world affairs, such as an international students' club on campus, United Nations Day activities, and international travel, seminars, and institutes; (4) provide a friendly arena for the scholarly consideration of controversial issues in world affairs; (5) create an opportunity for students to take a part of their academic work outside the United States.

As off-campus services to the community and region, Group III suggested that colleges (1) serve as a resource for schools and community groups by supplying leadership and teaching materials; (2) establish a world affairs reading room where significant documents and books would be available for loan or sale; (3) be alert to what citizens and communities are doing in international understanding and make this known by every available means—press, radio, TV, exhibits at fairs, etc.; (4) encourage organization of "world affairs" study groups, such as the Foreign Policy Association's "Great Decisions" groups, in all communities.

The case so convincingly made by Group III for university involvement in world affairs was heartily endorsed by Wellman's Group IV as a full and complete justification for its own central recommendation: massive financing of such participation by government.

The world position of the United States requires a far greater understanding of the economic, cultural, and political systems of other parts of the world. The need is urgent to understand more about the emerging nations, not as potential allies or enemies in some war that should not happen, but as potential markets, as sources of raw materials, and, above all, as groups of human individuals who have interest and challenge in their own right.

Aside from self-interest and short-term objectives and benefits, we need to do something about overseas matters in terms of basic principle. . . . Both "universal humanism" and the new world that is developing need re-emphasis for the domestic students who are in our charge in our own intellectual communities.

The Federal government has both *opportunity* and *obligation* to move further into international educational programs in a revolutionary kind of way. If it made sense to do so in the Land-Grant movement of 1862, it certainly makes sense to do so with an appropriate new kind of "revolution" in our own time. When one thinks of this particular juncture in history, he realizes that never again will any country be in such an advantageous position to shape the leadership of much of the world, to affect rising new nations and their economies, and to influence prevailing philosophies and international relationships.

It almost goes without saying, the Wellman group's report continued, that the educational revolution that started with the Morrill Act has deep implications for the development of international educational relations. In pursuit of this point it quoted Russell I. Thackrey, executive secretary of the Land-Grant association, who said in a speech at the University of Delaware in 1961:

It is no exaggeration to say that in all those countries of the free world which are striving toward a better life for their people, for the establishment of an educational and economic basis on which democracy can exist, the idea of the Land-Grant university is America's most popular export.

It is the results of this university-based, nationwide program of *instruction,* of *research* to find new knowledge, and *service* to bring it into practical application so as to improve the standards of living of the people, that account for the eagerness with which foreign countries seek to adapt the Land-Grant system to their own needs.

The Morrill legislation and subsequent agricultural legislation, Group IV declared,

may well serve as models for the development of international programs. The cooperative principle of Federal-State-local action should be further built into our international programs. The partnership of Federal government with participating state universities and colleges should be preserved. The ideal of teaching-research-adult education should be projected even further into this area of international studies. . . .

We need programs that are bold, imaginative, massive and *costly*. To have impact, in face of the immediate urgency, the programs must be conceived along a broad front; they must involve thousands and tens of thousands of people, U.S. nationals and those of other countries.

Just how *costly* these programs should be, the group did not explore at this point. It made estimates later in discussing the various specific programs considered by the other groups, and these estimates will be cited at appropriate points in the succeeding three chapters.

In any case, Group III emphasized, "if public education looks to the federal government for the stability of long-range programs, on its side education must accept responsibility for full involvement. . . . The Land-Grant colleges and universities have devoted substantial interest and resources to the federal-state partnership in service to agriculture. So must it be in international programs."

In the past, Wellman and his fellows pointed out, "pursuit of national objectives in international education has occasionally reduced universities to handmaidens of such objectives, sometimes to the detriment of the scholarly community and the services it can properly perform." Where this has happened, in their opinion, it has been by default of the universities in failing to "provide enlightened leadership" and in allowing themselves to be used by government rather than insisting on partnership status. As Group II put it: "American education will have to transcend the present limited aims . . . of technical assistance as the government defines it."

Just where to draw the line in all this, however, is in many cases admittedly perplexing. President Henry of Illinois, in his summary address at Kansas City, referred to "the uncertain alignment between the cosmopolitan responsibilities of scholarship and the exigencies of national foreign policy" and enjoined his listeners: "Essentially, how this alignment is made is a question of institutional and academic integrity and is not to be set aside quickly. We must always know when we are wearing our academic robes and when we are being garbed for diplomacy and decide for ourselves when the two are interchangeable."

CHAPTER FIVE

University Projects Overseas

"Many underdeveloped countries, including my own, India, have an existing system of university education, but the fact remains that this system does not meet the needs of our people. We want a more dynamic approach—something nearer the aspirations of the bulk of our people—and it is this spirit of service to the community, a spirit introduced in your country by the Land-Grant college, that we would like to foster in our country."

The speaker was K. A. P. Stevenson, vice chancellor of Uttar Pradesh Agricultural University, who served as one of four "discussants" of the report of International Study Group I at Kansas City.

The topic to which Group I, headed by Professor H. W. Hannah of Illinois, addressed itself, was: "The Special Role of Land-Grant Colleges and State Universities in Meeting the Needs of Developing Nations."

The Hannah group recognized that the needs of developing nations might be met through any number of channels, but it "assumed that with but a few exceptions personnel of Land-Grant universities on assignment abroad will be working in or in cooperation with educational institutions in the host country."

Stevenson assumed likewise, and to him there was no question of the "special role" these people and their universities must play. "You will bear the burden," he told his listeners, "because we want the sort of assistance that only the Land-Grant colleges can provide.

"We want your know-how in bringing the results of science to every farm and to every household. We want to give the same opportunities to the sons and daughters of our farmers and industrial classes that you gave to yours, and we want to adopt the methods which you have perfected."

Stevenson's prediction that "you will bear the burden" is, as a matter of record, already well toward realization. Heavy Land-Grant involvement in institution-building overseas began, in fact, in response to President Truman's historic "Point IV" speech in 1947. Inspired by the vision of service to struggling new nations which the speech presented, President John A. Hannah of Michigan State University and other Land-Grant leaders proposed that the Land-Grant association write Mr. Truman, saying "Here is something we can really take part in with great enthusiasm." The association sent this letter, and Land-Grant institutions soon found themselves deep in the program of the Technical Cooperation Administration, a lineal ancestor of today's Agency for International Development.

The whole Land-Grant concept was so obviously suited to what TCA was attempting to do that a Land-Grant man, President Henry Garland Bennett of Oklahoma Agricultural and Mechanical College (now Oklahoma State University), was named its first administrator.

Bennett was killed in an airplane crash while on duty abroad, but not before his own institution had undertaken the first major TCA educational project—an agricultural school in Ethiopia. The school was at the secondary level but, as its first class moved through, Oklahoma A & M was already at work helping Ethiopia build its Imperial Agricultural University. Today both school and university are thriving concerns.

About the same time that Oklahoma A & M was starting work in Ethiopia, the Army contracted with Michigan

State to build a Land-Grant-type university in Okinawa, which it was then occupying. This has been functioning for several years now as the University of Ryukyus, the first higher educational institution in that part of the world.

As other instances of such Land-Grant work abroad, Nebraska helped to build Ataturk University in Turkey, which graduated its first class in 1962; Purdue developed Taiwan Engineering College; and Cornell aided in establishment of the Agricultural College of the Philippines at Los Banos.

Uttar Pradesh Agricultural University, Stevenson's own institution, is another product of Land-Grant effort—by the University of Illinois—in building a new university from scratch.

Table I gives a breakdown by institution, field of program (agriculture, engineering, etc.), region, and country of projects being carried on under AID (ICA) contracts as of June 30, 1962.

TABLE I. *Land-Grant Institutions Under Contract* [a]
with Countries Abroad, [b] *August 1962*

Land-Grant Institution	Field of Program	Contract Dates
	AFRICA	
Ethiopia		
Oklahoma State University (Stillwater)	Agriculture	1952-63
Utah State University (Logan)	Education	1962-65
Liberia		
Cornell University (Ithaca, N.Y.)	Education	1962-65
Nigeria		
University of California (Berkeley)	Education (2 contracts)	1961-64
Michigan State University (East Lansing)	Education	1960-64
Ohio State University (Columbus)	Education	1958-65

[a] Contracts negotiated since 1958 are under AID only.
[b] As listed June 30, 1962, by Contract Services Division, Agency for International Development, Department of State, Washington, D.C.

Land-Grant Institution	Field of Program	Contract Dates
Tanganyika		
West Virginia University (Morgantown)	Education, Agriculture	1962
Tunisia		
Texas A & M College System (College Station)	Agriculture	1962
Uganda		
University of Masschusetts (Amherst)	Education	1961-62
Totals: 9 institutions in 6 countries	2 major fields	10 contracts, 1952-65

FAR EAST

Cambodia		
University of Georgia (Athens)	Agriculture	1960-63
China		
Michigan State University (East Lansing)	Vocational Agriculture, Education	1960-64
Indonesia		
University of California (Berkeley)	Medical Education	1959-64
University of California (Berkeley)	Engineering	1957-63
University of Kentucky (Lexington)	Engineering	1956-63
University of Kentucky (Lexington)	Agriculture	1957-63
Philippines		
State University of New York (Albany)	Agriculture	1960-64
Thailand		
Colorado State University (Fort Collins)	Education (Engineering)	1959-63
University of Hawaii (Honolulu)	Vocational Industrial Education	1958-63
University of Hawaii (Honolulu)	Education, Agriculture	1962-65
Vietnam		
University of Georgia (Athens)	Agriculture	1960-62
Totals: 7 institutions in 6 countries	5 major fields	11 contracts, 1956-65

Land-Grant Institution	*Field of Program*	*Contract Dates*
	LATIN AMERICA	

Brazil

University of California (Berkeley)	Community Development	1962-65
Michigan State University (East Lansing)	Business Administration	1953-62
Michigan State University (East Lansing)	Business Administration	1959-64
Michigan State University (East Lansing)	Audio-Visual	1960-63
Purdue University (Lafayette, Ind.)	Agriculture, Home Economics	1958-64

Chile

Cornell University (Ithaca, N.Y.)	Labor Affairs	1959-63

Costa Rica

Louisiana State University (Baton Rouge)	Medical Education	1959-63

Guatemala

University of Kentucky (Lexington)	Agriculture	1957-63

Panama

University of Tennessee (Knoxville)	Public Administration	1955-64

Paraguay

Montana State College (Bozeman)	Agriculture	1960-63

Peru

Iowa State University (Ames)	Agriculture	1961-62
North Carolina State College (Raleigh)	Agriculture	1961-63

Uruguay

Iowa State University (Ames)	Education	1962

Totals: 10 institutions in 8 countries	9 major fields	13 contracts, 1953-65

	NEAR EAST AND SOUTH ASIA	

Afghanistan

University of Wyoming (Laramie)	Agriculture	1954-64

Land-Grant Institution	Field of Program	Contract Dates
India		
University of Illinois (Urbana)	Agriculture	1959-63
University of Illinois (Urbana)	Agriculture	1955-63
University of Illinois (Urbana)	Education, Engineering	1959-63
Kansas State University (Manhattan)	Agriculture	1956-63
Michigan State University (East Lansing)	Education, Engineering	1960-63
University of Missouri (Columbia)	Agriculture	1957-63
Ohio State University (Columbus)	Education	1956-63
Ohio State University (Columbus)	Agriculture	1955-63
University of Tennessee (Knoxville)	Agriculture	1956-63
University of Wisconsin (Madison)	Education, Engineering	1959-63
Iran		
Utah State University (Logan)	Agriculture	1958-63
Jordan		
University of Nebraska (Lincoln)	Education	1962
Pakistan		
University of Hawaii (Honolulu)	Vocational Industrial Education	1961-64
Colorado State University (Fort Collins)	Education, Engineering, Agriculture, Home Economics	1958-63
Texas A & M College System (College Station)	Education, Business Administration, Agriculture, Home Economics	1958-63
Washington State University (Pullman)	Education, Business Administration, Agriculture, Engineering, Home Economics	1954-63
Turkey		
Cornell University (Ithaca, N.Y.)	Public and Business Administration	1961-64

Land-Grant Institution	Field of Program	Contract Dates
University of Nebraska (Lincoln)	Agriculture, Engineering, Business Administration, Education	1958-62
Totals: 15 institutions in 6 countries	6 major fields	19 contracts, 1954-64

Summary Totals: contracts, 53
countries, 26
Land-Grant institutions, 27

In all, 27 Land-Grant colleges and universities were conducting 53 projects in 26 countries—a healthy and well-distributed share of the 107 projects being carried on in 37 countries by a total of 65 American universities, public and private. Of the Land-Grant contracts, 25 were in education, 26 in agriculture, 2 in public administration, 8 in engineering, and 6 in business administration.

Not all overseas activities are government-financed. Foundations also are involved. The Ford Foundation, for example, was involved in the Los Banos agricultural college and supports a regional agricultural assistance program in India, in which several university teams are at work. The Carnegie Corporation finances an African program. In all, under government and other auspices, 2,500 faculty members from 433 U.S. institutions were on assignment in 90 countries in 1961-62.

Eight of the 13 institutions reporting more than 30 faculty members abroad were Land-Grant universities. Michigan State alone had 222, or 10 per cent of the total.

Within this numerical framework, the Hannah group proceeded to examine how a Land-Grant university (or, actually, any university) might be of greatest service to an overseas people through their own college or university.

The first principle it set forth—and with unshakable emphasis—was that the American institution itself must be involved from top to bottom in the project.

And this implies an involvement beyond the purely academic. How effective would our agricultural colleges have been in promoting the national purpose regarding agriculture if their staff members had not been constantly immersed in the problems of farmers? And who will deny that the scores of countries in the world with peoples whose needs are far greater than those of the American farmer of a century ago, offer a wider challenge, and one which it is even more important to meet, for the peace of the world may depend on it? . . .

The increasing numbers of foreign scholars coming to our universities for the express purpose of perfecting their ability to deal with problems at home cast a different light on the responsibility of the university toward them. Other things being equal, these foreign scholars will benefit most by studying in a university which has been involved in educational assistance to either their country or one with similar problems. Certainly a university with several hundred foreign students should not feel comfortable in these times if it has never been involved in a country abroad, or at least if it does not have a reasonable number of staff members with foreign experience.

To all this, Stevenson, "presenting the views of the recipient," was ready to attest:

Involvement should be an all-university affair, involving the administration, the business office and the specialized colleges. We really need your help in all facets of university life, not just in specialized skills, if we are to introduce the spirit of the Land-Grant college system. . . . We need help in such things as registration, in our student work program, in teaching aids, library, and we can only obtain this help if the president's office, the provost's office, the college of agriculture, the college of veterinary medicine, the business office and everybody, in fact the whole university, is involved.

Before becoming involved at all, however, Group I cautioned, each university should examine its motives for involvement. Some institutions, it observed, have entered into overseas projects just to get aboard the bandwagon, or for prestige purposes, or because a certain faculty member was "high" on the idea, or simply because it did not know how to refuse a request from the government. Rejecting all these as valid reasons, it declared: "A genuine interest in broadening the research and service horizon, a real concern about our nation's impact in the world, and the desire to serve mankind all seem more cogent. . . . An institution which becomes involved on the spur of the moment through acceptance of a request farmed out to one of its colleges cannot possibly bring into play all the resources it could and should marshal if the program were less hurriedly involved and a continuing long-range objective were established."

What can happen in the absence of full commitment and thorough understanding of motives was tellingly illustrated in Hannah's own report after two years in the mid-1950's during which he served as group leader of the University of Illinois team which was at that time getting the Uttar Pradesh project under way. Quoted by Group I in its own report, here is what it said:

The fact that a positive program was not well laid out in advance at the university has been most discouraging to many of the people who had to work with the program. Without a well-laid plan at the university it has been difficult to get the enthusiasm and cooperation of department heads and others, and recruitment of staff members for assignment in India has been a problem. Of the seven specialists recruited by the University of Illinois, I was the only one from the home campus; five were from other states. This in a large measure defeats the "institution-to-institution" idea and tends to leave the university primarily a recruiting and purchasing agent for the program and a reception center for participants from India.

The home university should draw up a plan to meet the requirements of the entire contract. This should be done with the advice and help of administrators, department heads, and other personnel involved in the program. Among the points that should be determined are ways to supply needed specialists, guide Indian participants, and take care of purchases and record keeping. Ideally each department head would establish communication with counterpart departments in the region where the university is cooperating.

Finally the university should make its foreign programs more a part of its total educational effort—philosophically as well as materially. Without this attitude, it might easily appear that the contract operation is a responsibility which the university feels honor bound to discharge, but about which it has developed no great enthusiasm or vision.

This report, it should be noted, was written early in the game. By 1961, Stevenson was able to say at Kansas City that commitment in depth, from the president's office on down, "is the position of the University of Illinois."

By and large, Group I felt, universities have been too little involved in planning ICA-AID programs and too little freed to carry out the plan once it is evolved. The group's report said:

This stems in part from the failure of Congress to provide a charter, so to speak, and perhaps even a formula for the granting of funds as it did in the case of agricultural research and agricultural extension work. In the beginning universities were brought into the program of ICA more for the purpose of helping that agency solve some of its recruitment and personnel problems than for the unique contribution which these institutions could make.

Although AID is now conscious of the contribution which our universities can make, it is, nevertheless, still wedded to certain established ways and procedures which have stemmed from administrative regulation and executive orders. We recognize that this condition has resulted in part from "growing pains," and we hasten to say that universities have also suffered the shortcomings which stem from newness of program and inexperience.

Rather than emphasize the negative aspects of past performance, we would encourage meaningful reorganization by government, legislative recognition of this new dimension for our Land-Grant institutions, and more serious appraisal by the universities of what they are doing.

That the U.S. government is not totally unaware of the quandaries which the group cited was made clear in the remarks of James Grant of AID, who also served as a "discussant" at Kansas City. Grant opened this portion of his remarks by saying that it is clear that "major changes" will have to be made in what Land-Grant institutions are doing abroad. But, he quickly added:

It is also clear that this is not something that you can hold the Land-Grant colleges to on their own responsibility. The U.S. government has a major role here, just as it did in 1862, when the Land-Grant concept was developed.

On the government side, we really did not seriously get into the development business in the decade of the 50's. Our programs then were essentially crisis-oriented, as those of you who worked in the programs abroad recognize. They were on a hand-to-mouth basis, with relatively little in terms of comprehensive goals and long-term programs.

Toward the end of the decade we moved into increased emphasis on development, but I would say that it was only in the past year that we crossed the watershed on this.

This new program recognizes several things for the first time:

First, that development, as distinguished from the past emphasis on short-term crisis situations, is the principal preoccupation of the aid business.

Second, that this is not a two-year or three-year process but that we must talk in terms of decades or more.

Third, that this takes far more resources. Over the two-year period '62-'63, the U.S. government is putting more than a billion dollars into the aid program.

Fourth, that development is not just the increase of productivity, but that integrally related to and part of this is education and social development—that you can't have successful development without this.

Finally, it recognizes the fact that we need a far better organization to do this job in the United States government and, of great importance, that we really don't have the answers yet, that we need a great deal of research if we are to find the answers.

My own feeling is that a tremendous change in dimension, in scope and quality of our Land-Grant college programs overseas is yet to come, and that the equivalent of the 1862 movement of Land-Grant colleges at home is something yet for the future.

Further thoughts as to the government's proper role and **responsibilities** in assistance to foreign universities were set forth by Wellman's Study Group IV:

At the present, federal appropriations to assist in the development of foreign universities amount to approximately $40,000,-000 per year and are mainly devoted to professional areas and applied fields. To date, ICA-financed university contracts total $101,000,000. Fifty-six universities have undertaken 100 contracts in 37 countries.[1]

Despite this substantial record of accomplishment and of international cooperation, we note that the program has not yet reached at least forty other non-European countries. . . .

Assistance programs to foreign universities should be substantially enlarged (on the order of two to three times) and should include more countries and more disciplines, the humanities and social sciences, as well as the natural sciences and professional fields.

Appropriate financial arrangements by the Federal government with participating colleges and universities should contemplate long-term (six to 10-year) institutional grants, so arranged that the universities could operate under their own procedures. Grants should cover the *full costs* of participation, including overhead. Grants should allow participating universities to achieve staffing formulae that would, in effect, provide an excess, so that faculty members could be rotated on foreign assignment without diminishing instruction and research at home.

The number of participating universities and colleges should be substantially increased so that the program (and the burden) is spread evenly and widely. There should be concentration of university effort; insofar as possible, a single university should specialize on a single country. In fullest degree, the program may result in a university having a "branch" campus abroad, with free interchange of students and faculty.

The Land-Grant concept was singled out for particular notice by Group IV. "It should be transplanted abroad wherever the environment and conditions appear promising," it recommended, and "university programs abroad should likewise include the Land-Grant triad: teaching, research, and extension."

Realistically, Group IV conceded, "many of the emerging

[1] The figures in this paragraph were taken from the ICA report of March 31, 1961, the latest available at the time. In the September 30, 1962, AID report, total contracts had risen to nearly $116,800,000, with 65 universities reported involved in 111 projects, although the number of countries, because of expiration of contracts, had declined to 35. These later figures do not significantly alter Group IV's conclusions.

nations will have greater need for assistance in the development of two-year lower-division colleges, teachers colleges, and technical institutes," rather than universities, at first.

"To this end," it continued, "the foreign assistance program should contemplate making greater use of U.S. state, community and two-year colleges. On the other hand, as foreign educational institutions develop and mature, they may be expected to take over the education of their own nationals, first at undergraduate level, eventually at the graduate level, ultimately diminishing the need for extensive instruction of foreign students and faculty in the U.S."

Again realistically, despite its call for a doubling or tripling of government support of overseas university activity, Group IV recognized that "funds alone will not insure success." The final paragraphs of its remarks in this area underlined what Group I had said: that deep involvement by American universities is essential. The paragraph read:

A university stance is required which clearly stimulates and challenges bright young professors to make intellectual commitments to international affairs, studies and programs for substantial periods of time. It is more than the encouragement of leaves for international study or the use of federal money to build new programs; it is a willingness . . . to permit and encourage the best people to take such assignments, and an eagerness to support new courses and curricula which better reflect the needs of American society today and tomorrow. It is shown by the pride which the university president and dean express to the faculty and to the public for success in these areas.

The physical and financial wherewithal will clearly help. But there are things that can be done short of such financial commitments—things which our institutions must do anyway because our society needs them badly. Moreover, some shifts in emphasis now, some steps to promote greater faculty interest on a long-term basis will help bring the shifts in financial allocations into being.

In short, the ideas and attitudes need to be emphasized along with budgetary commitments. Much can be done without any change in total budget.

CHAPTER SIX

The Foreign Student, Scholar, and Trainee in the United States

"It was 10 below zero the day I arrived on campus; 78 hours before, I had left the tropical heat of Africa. I had had very little contact with any Americans. I felt insecure in my ability to communicate in English, and I had no real concept of the social and educational environment into which I was catapulted so abruptly."

The misery expressed in this extract from a report by an African student underlines the contention of International Study Group II that "the foreign student on our campuses is not just like any other student." The fact that this young man had been educated in a former French colony, in a school conducted on the French model, totally unlike American schools, heightened the contrast.

There were about 58,000 foreign students on American campuses in 1961-62, and it was to them and their problems—in particular to the problems of the approximately 16,250 on Land-Grant campuses—that Study Group II addressed itself. Its topic, explored under the chairmanship of Dean John McConnell of Cornell University's School of Industrial and Labor Relations, was "Steps Needed to Improve or Develop Programs to Meet the Needs of Foreign Scholars, Students, and Trainees."

Not all of the foreign students who arrive on Land-Grant and other campuses each year present such extremes as the

63

freezing young African, but enough of them come close to it in climatic, social, economic, educational, or cultural terms to create a real challenge—a challenge that Group II found is too seldom met. "There is mounting evidence," the group reported, "that with many of these students we are failing to make friends for the United States. . . . The dilemma arising from this condition is particularly distressing because educational exchange has become an important aspect of national policy, particularly as regards students from Asia, Africa, and Latin America."

As they do in the case of American students, the Land-Grant institutions carry far more than their proportionate share of the enrollment of foreign students. Numbering only 68, about 3½ per cent of all American institutions of higher education, they enroll about a fourth of all foreign students and are hosts to 39 per cent of all foreign professors and advanced research scholars. Table II shows how these persons are distributed among all institutions and

TABLE II. *Educational Exchange—U.S. Colleges and Universities, 1961-62* [a]

	All U.S. Colleges and Universities	Land-Grant Institutions [b]
Number of institutions reporting foreign students (149 countries)	1,798	62
Number of foreign students		
Undergraduate	29,376	5,734
Graduate	24,624	9,504
Special or unclassified	4,086	1,028
Totals	58,086	16,266
Number of visiting foreign senior scholars	5,530	2,229
Number of U.S. faculty abroad	2,427	859

[a] Source: *Open Doors 1962*—Report on International Exchange, Institute of International Education, New York.
[b] Six Land-Grant institutions (Alabama A & M College, Delaware State College, Fort Valley [Ga.] State College, Maryland State College, Lincoln [Mo.] University, and Langston [Okla.] University) failed to report.

Land-Grant institutions, and Table III shows the number of foreign students at each Land-Grant institution which enrolls any such students.

TABLE III. *Foreign Students Enrolled in Land-Grant Institutions, 1961-1962* [a]

Land-Grant Institution	Under-graduate	Graduate	Special or Un-classified	Total
Auburn University (Alabama)	45	25	9	79
University of Alaska	15	6		21
University of Arizona	167	90	20	277
Agricultural, Mechanical and Normal College (Arkansas)	14			14
University of Arkansas	25	25	6	56
University of California	800	1,676	58	2,534
Colorado State University	50	66		116
University of Connecticut	16	29	1	46
University of Delaware	19	48	3	70
Florida Agricultural and Mechanical University	5			5
University of Florida	177	103	17	297
Georgia Institute of Technology	136	50	6	192
University of Georgia	25	44	21	90
University of Hawaii	144	216	70	430
University of Idaho	12	10		22
University of Illinois	389	717	32	1,138
Purdue University (Indiana)	156	390	9	555
Iowa State University	98	173	17	288
Kansas State University	122	231	10	363
Kentucky State College	3			3
University of Kentucky	41	66	7	114
Louisiana State University	200	127	8	335
University of Maine	20	13	6	39
University of Maryland	88	250	15	353
Massachusetts Institute of Technology	218	500	54	772
University of Massachusetts	10	55	2	67
Michigan State University	191	368	88	647
University of Minnesota	161	735	143	1,039

[a] Source: *Open Doors 1962*—Report on International Exchange, Institute of International Education, New York.

Land-Grant Institution	Under-gradu-ate	Gradu-ate	Special or Un-classified	Total
Alcorn Agricultural and Mechan-				
ical College (Mississippi)	2	1		3
Mississippi State University	27	21	3	51
University of Missouri	229	244	23	496
Montana State College	137	22	1	160
University of Nebraska	111	118	3	232
University of Nevada	26	12	1	39
University of New Hampshire	30	16	5	51
Rutgers University (New Jersey)	28	139	16	183
New Mexico State University	63	13	12	88
Cornell University (New York)	171	557	30	758
Agricultural and Technical				
College of North Carolina	30	1	11	42
North Carolina State College	97	162	24	283
North Dakota State University	44	17	1	62
Ohio State University	129	372	40	541
Oklahoma State University	254	187	43	484
Oregon State University	88	112	6	206
Pennsylvania State University	44	156	23	223
University of Puerto Rico	106	43	56	205
University of Rhode Island	20	42	1	63
Clemson Agricultural College				
(South Carolina)	16	3	1	20
South Carolina State College	1			1
South Dakota State College	35	12		47
Tennessee Agricultural and				
Industrial State University	6	1		7
University of Tennessee	12	12	1	25
Agricultural and Mechanical				
College of Texas	117	88	11	216
Prairie View Agricultural and				
Mechanical College (Texas)	2	3	1	6
Utah State University	141	78	9	228
University of Vermont	8	21	3	32
Virginia Polytechnic Institute	26	116	3	145
Virginia State College	1			1
Washington State University	141	96	2	239
West Virginia University	24	32	6	62
University of Wisconsin	188	768	90	1,046
University of Wyoming	33	26		59
Totals	5,734	9,504	1,028	16,266

Of all foreign students, about 10 per cent, some 5,500, were financed solely by the U.S. government, and an additional 1,150 were financed jointly by the U.S. government and private agencies. Exclusively private support accounted for 22,000; another 17,500 were self-supported; foreign governments financed 2,829. Something over 500 were supported jointly by foreign governments and private agencies.

Foreign students represent slightly less than 1.5 per cent of the total enrollment in all U.S. institutions of higher learning. In Land-Grant institutions they represent 2.1 per cent, and in the opinion of Group II it is only fitting that they should. It said in its report:

> By their nature and experience in devising educational programs to meet the economic conditions of the states at the time of their origin, Land-Grant institutions are better equipped in general to meet the needs of foreign students than the average American private college and university, founded upon the base of a strong liberal arts college. . . .
> The Land-Grant institution has been an integral part of a growing democracy. It was designed to break the rigid mold of a classical and traditional curriculum; it was founded to meet the expanding need for education of a rising industrial class of people; it sought to add a practical dimension to the structure of a liberal education. These are the identical needs of today's developing nations, whose elite classes have enjoyed the benefits of a cultural education in the best private universities of the Western world, but whose general population has been denied the opportunity to learn even the elementary subjects of reading, writing, and arithmetic.
> The advantage of Land-Grant institutions as centers for the education of foreign students rests not alone on their history and philosophy, but on the close relationship of their current operations to the needs of foreign countries. Land-Grant institutions have developed qualified staff, scientific knowledge, and research competence in agricultural and technological fields which are all-important to developing economies. They have had broad experience in conducting short-term, intensive training programs, and a large proportion of their manpower and financial resources is devoted to adult education.
> The educational programs of Land-Grant institutions are

available to all groups in society so long as the educational need is real and of public interest. Current problems of scientific, technical or social nature are accepted as the targets of educational effort in Land-Grant institutions.

Thus, Group II concluded, through purpose, history, and resources, the Land-Grant institutions are probably the best qualified among our educational institutions to meet the appeal of the developing nations. "Nevertheless," it continued,

these institutions are at something of a disadvantage in responding to this appeal. In the nations of Asia, Africa, and South America, education must inevitably be looked upon as an instrument of national development. It cannot be an end in itself. The Land-Grant institution, while stressing the importance of practical subjects, emphasizes an individual approach to education, and the curriculum provides a greater latitude of individual choice of subjects and devotion to liberal study than the pressing need for well-trained men and women in the new nations of the world can permit.

Furthermore, our educational system with its leisurely pace, tolerance of an educational "smorgasbord" approach, and devotion to cultural studies as part of education for living, may not be efficient enough or purposeful enough to meet the needs of the struggling economies of Asia, Africa, and South America. They desperately need the strong support of trained minds and skilled hands immediately.

That this immediate need for "trained minds and skilled hands" does indeed create a dilemma for the Land-Grant, as well as other, institutions was pointed up in a report by the Institute of International Education in 1955. The Institute, a private, nonprofit organization which administers numerous exchange programs, analyzed the stated objectives of various public and private sponsors of student exchanges. In the order in which they were stated most frequently, these objectives were: (1) to promote international understanding and good will among the peoples of the world as a contribution to peace; (2) to develop friends and supporters for the United States by giving persons from other countries a better understanding of the life and culture of the United States; (3) to contribute to the economic, social, or political development of other countries; (4) to aid in the education or professional development of outstanding individuals; (5) to advance knowledge throughout the world for the general welfare of mankind.

When the stated objectives of foreign students were analyzed, the same goals appeared in almost inverse order. Most students put No. 4 first, indicating that they came to the United States to advance their personal and professional development. But, Group II reiterated:

> The task of American higher education for all foreign students is more basic than teaching them only how to build bridges, only how better to till the fields, only how to edit books, only how to teach reading to U.S. third grade pupils, or only how to balance a ledger or do a manpower survey.
>
> In fact, to let them depart with degrees signifying technological proficiency and nothing else is to fail them and give communism the rebound chance to catch "liberally illiterate men." For students from new countries and from countries still in the womb of independence, U.S. higher education has the task not only of exposing them to our technological knowledge but to the universal humanism found in a liberal approach to western knowledge, thought and experience. Through this approach foreign students may acquire an appreciation of the dignity and necessity of work and of the responsibility for public service which their educational advantage places upon them.

Within this wide context of what foreign students, and their governments, want and expect of American universities versus what the universities want to give them, Group II identified many subissues. Among them were the questions of whether assignment of foreign students to universities should be more carefully controlled and whether academic programs should be modified to suit the needs and backgrounds of these students, the matter of easing their social relations, the touchy problem of English language competence, and special advisory services.

Examining, first, the assignment of students, the group wrote:

In the light of weaknesses and failures in the program, several questions have been raised concerning improving the situation through more controls in the assignment of foreign students, exercised outside the individual institutions. A good deal of structuring now occurs through the IIE, various government agencies, and the educational and cultural offices of foreign embassies. But it has been suggested that the education and training of sponsored students at least be regionalized; that is, students from one country or group of geographically or culturally allied countries be sent only to certain designated universities.

While such an arrangement has obvious advantages, notably in the degree of specialization that would result, it would reduce substantially one of the major benefits of educational exchange, the cross-fertilization that results from having students from many countries and cultures on the same campus. The normal tendency of foreign students to associate with their fellow countrymen—a tendency that generally should be opposed—would be intensified.

It has also been proposed that our exchange program might be improved if certain institutions were identified and especially designated for educational work of certain kinds. If this process would result in greater concentration of foreign students in a few universities, it too would be undesirable. . . . All foreign students, particularly those from non-European countries, consider prestige in the selection of an American institution, but the university with the most prestigious department in some field may not offer the student the most meaningful education. He may get more attention and quite possibly better training in a smaller institution. It would be better if the total number of foreign students in Land-Grant institutions were less concentrated. . . .

A suggestion of a different type proposes increasing the number of direct institution-to-institution relationships. Historically, certain private colleges or universities had such relationships with American mission colleges abroad, as Yale-in-China. In more recent times, Land-Grant universities have established similar relationships. . . .

There are real advantages to such relationships, especially in connection with the exchange of both students and faculty. A special sense of mutual responsibility develops and continuity of interest is maintained. Its chief limitation is that it narrows the international interests of the American institution to the home country of the associated institution. If foreign students from all countries are welcomed to the American university, however, the danger of narrow interest is offset.

The total program of educational exchange, however, will not show great improvement, Group II felt, until the educational experience in American colleges and universities meets more satisfactorily the needs of the individual foreign student. The group defined the issue thus:

The practical question is simply whether there should be more or less prescribed programs and university designations for foreign students than now exist. The arguments for and against course prescription for foreign students are similar to those heard in debates on American university curricula generally. The unique factor in this aspect of the dilemma is the economic necessity for specialized knowledge and skill in the foreign student's homeland. What is our obligation as educators to assure foreign countries that their precious resource of trained manpower will not be dissipated in interesting but irrelevant study programs here in the United States?

The administrative organization of the foreign student program on the individual campus must be designed to contribute to the educational aims of the foreign student, however they may be described. . . . It has been suggested that all foreign student affairs—academic, financial, and social—in Land-Grant institutions be placed under the direction of a single high university administrative officer, who could coordinate foreign student activities both within the university and between the university and outside agencies. This group would prefer a strengthening of interest and competence in handling foreign student problems in the existing functional offices of university administration—financial, admissions, academic, and student relations and services.

The social relations of foreign students, superficially important as they at first might seem, were regarded by Group II as of critical importance. In its own words:

The moment the newly arrived foreign student sets foot in his host country, his attitudes and values are challenged by those of the new environment. How any one student will cope with the problem of adjustment is one of the great unknowns. Lacking an easy solution to problems of adjustment, greater emphasis must be given to improving the techniques and methods which will permit a selection of those persons "most likely to succeed," and then provide qualified personnel and adequate facilities to assist in the process of fitting a foreign student into a new and very complex life.

Though the problems of adjustment are often similar, the foreign student on our campuses is not just like any other student. Every one of them comes from a unique set of circumstances.

Competence in English is often the key factor in the student's social adjustment. Lacking ability to communicate effectively may bring about a withdrawal from contact with others which may be interpreted as avoidance, aloofness, or indifference.

An important aid in this particular phase of adjustment, the group reported from its own firsthand knowledge, is to help the student develop "at least one warm and reliable relationship" with an understanding fellow student, for example, or with a friendly faculty member or a host family in the community.

Two other likely sources of social difficulty for foreign students, the group said, are relationships with the opposite sex and racial discrimination. On neither score was it very optimistic of early or easy solution. On the former, it noted that "dating" customs in many foreign lands vary widely from our own, and inasmuch as these are deeply entrenched in culture there is small chance of doing much about a foreign student's viewpoint in this respect in the relatively short time he is on an American campus. On the latter, it concluded only that "despite our best efforts, African students will undoubtedly encounter some form of racial discrimination."

English language difficulties, of course, are critical not only in social relationships but in the foreign student's academic pursuits. "We must depend upon English as the language of instruction," Group II concluded after examining proposals to offer instruction in foreign languages—and finding them "absurd."

Most institutions endeavor to secure information concerning proficiency in English before admitting foreign students; most also provide special instruction in English for the foreign student after his arrival on the campus. But the condition is cause for real concern.

Certification by personnel in American consulates concerning the proficiency in English of students being admitted has proved unreliable. Those institutions having contracts with ICA (AID) have found that recommendations from officials in United States Overseas Missions are not reliable. Certification by foreign professors has proved unsatisfactory. Even evaluation by professors of the American institutions, who happen to be abroad at the time, is inadequate to meet the need. In numerous cases American professors have been instrumental in bringing to their own institution foreign students whose competence in the fields of specialization may be high but whose proficiency in English is woefully inadequate.

It is highly desirable to test the foreign student's proficiency in English before he is admitted to an American institution; the testing should be done abroad.

The University of Michigan has established a wide network of English testing centers in almost every country, and has developed standardized tests, but Group II reported that apparently the Michigan test is very effective only in screening those with a high proficiency in the use of English and those with a very low proficiency—"not nearly so accurate with respect to the large number of students who fall between the extremes."

English for foreign students has become a major enterprise on most university campuses, but the group considered that, even so, "the problem of English language instruction has not been met," and added: "It is apparent that the Federal government should encourage a solution to the language problem by creating and financing enough language centers to give English language instruction to every foreign student coming to the United States to study —first, before he leaves his native land, and then in the United States, if additional instruction is necessary."

The final point which Group II examined within the larger context of effective relationships between university and foreign student was that of special on-campus services. "In any institution with more than a handful of foreign students," it said, "the special responsibility for them must be centered in a foreign student advisor." As an important qualification, the group added: "He must have adequate secretarial help and office space."

James M. Davis, foreign student advisor at the University of Michigan, who was one of the "discussants" of the group's report, recommended a full-time advisor with a full-time secretary and some paid student assistants for each 200 foreign students. Yet Homer Higbee of the Land-Grant Michigan State University had but recently published a survey which showed that 56.5 per cent of foreign student advisors had no help at all.

Moreover, the group declared, "the functions of the student advisor are seldom clearly defined. . . . Few of the present foreign student advisors sought this post; generally they were requested to accept this function while holding positions as deans, department heads, guidance directors or student counselors. . . . There is little question that in most Land-Grant institutions more assistance is needed in counseling foreign students."

The report noted that Congress has provided federal funds to help finance the specialized services needed by foreign students, and it urged that universities apply for these funds as "the only way needed services will be provided."

Not strictly a part of the university–foreign student relationship, at least while the student is on campus, but still vitally important in Group II's view, is the matter of providing some sort of "decompression chamber to ease the strains of going back into old patterns of life."

During the academic year 1960-61, the group noted, about two-thirds of all foreign students had been in the United States for three years or more—61 per cent of the Nigerian students, for example.

"The engineer who has become used to the theoretical

engineering problems and superb equipment of MIT," it continued, "may be chagrined on his return to Asia or Africa to find his big ideas utterly incompatible with the skills and resources of his city. . . . And what of those female foreign students who find the mobility, economic potential and prestige of the American woman so enviable as they contemplate a return to their own lands?"

The group called for "orientation in reverse" for homeward-bound foreign students. This, it said, "might recapitulate and interpret his experiences here, sort out from the total program the insights which were purely American and those which might be applicable at home."

One way to forestall the problem of the student returning home to situations widely different from what he has been experiencing in the United States—and a way that is rapidly gaining favorable attention—is what is called the "third country" plan. Under this plan foreign students might not be brought to the United States but supported in some other country, other than their own but where conditions are more like those to which they are accustomed.

The case for such a plan was outlined by President Renne of Montana State College, acting as a discussant of Group IV's paper at Kansas City. Renne, who had served two years as country director in the Philippines, one of the countries where his institution had been involved in technical and economic assistance, put it in these terms:

First of all, the conditions of learning and the over-all situation—economic, social and other situations—are more understandable, more comparable, more reconcilable, in many cases, with the condition of the student at that time of his development and maturity.

Second, it would be far less expensive.

Third, the type of education which would be available in a third country situation would be adequate in many, many situations, especially the undergraduate general type of education.

The advanced and specialized student is ordinarily ready, or more nearly ready, for conditions in the United States than the undergraduate. But even here there are several countries to which we could send students or to which students could go that would be as adequate, and in some cases more adequate, in some fields, than the United States.

Group IV's appraisal of government support of programs for the education of students from foreign nations began with this cogent statement:

In the opinion of this study group, expenditures to support foreign undergraduate and graduate students and faculty (and to provide assistance in the development of foreign universities) will most probably bring greater results per dollar of expenditure than some of our direct aid programs. The impression of the United States on the human resources of the world through a bold, all-out effort here could do more than all else put together—more for United States relations overseas, for our prestige and influence, for future leadership abroad, and for economic development overseas through competence and skill.

The group noted the probability that "leaders of the smaller and poorer nations will for some time be educated abroad," and pressed the view that "it is important that as many as possible be educated in the United States." It also, however, recommended attention to the third country idea as discussed by Renne.

In later discussion, too, Chairman Wellman emphasized the thought, which he described as "implicit" in Study Group IV's report, that "as soon as practicable, U.S. colleges and universities should get out of undergraduate training of foreign students."

The goal, Wellman said, "should be to develop foreign institutions to do the job, eventually even at the graduate level, at which time U.S. training of foreign graduate students would be the same as the normal scholarly exchange now enjoyed with the more mature educational institutions of the better developed countries."

Experience indicates that such an approach would be welcomed by the majority of foreign university educators. The rector of a leading South American university, visiting this country, told a state university president: "The best thing you can do for us is to work with us in our own countries as far as the mass of students is concerned. Train leaders here, yes, but help us at home with the mass of students."

With reference to the way things stand now, the Wellman group found much to be desired in federal support of foreign student programs. It noted first that the Foreign Assistance and the Mutual Exchange and Cultural Acts of 1961 provided for $296.5 million for assistance to other countries, including educational assistance, and for "educational exchanges . . . by financing studies, research and other educational activities for nationals of foreign countries in American schools and institutions of higher learning."

"These programs are aimed in the proper direction," it said, "but the federal government should go further. Appropriations should be larger for educational cooperation. Programs should be continuing and long-term, not subject to the political pressures of each congressional session. Programs should be focused more precisely on the emerging nations" (of the Near East, the Far East, Africa, and Central and South America).

The group recommended that the total of federally sponsored students (about 5,500 in 1961-62) "be immediately increased at least three fold, and possibly five fold, to a total of 15,000 to 25,000 persons."

To the extent to which the federal government sponsors foreign students and faculty, Group IV declared,

it should reimburse universities for all the costs of providing for their instruction, including capital outlay.

Government-sponsored foreign students and faculty should receive transportation and living expenses, and they should be free to elect their courses of study, not limited to professional and applied fields. Additionally, those who engage in teaching and research should be eligible to return periodically to the United States for refresher training.

Federal programs designed to bring short-term foreign

visitors to U.S. institutions of public higher education should provide for adequate reimbursement to participating institutions for all costs—direct or indirect—of receiving such visitors.

Endorsing Group II's proposal that the government should stand the cost of English language studies, better methods of selection, better counseling, and improved orientation for foreign students, Group IV proceeded to analyze the expenditures for educational and general purposes for a full-time student (not including medical students) by the University of California in 1960-61. Expenditures were:

Lower division (freshmen and sophomores)	$1,112
Upper division (juniors and seniors)	1,738
Graduate school	2,703

On the basis of 34 per cent lower division, 40 per cent upper division, and 26 per cent graduate school students, the ratio found at California, the "weighted average" cost was $1,770.

California had about 2,000 foreign students in 1960-61. Thus, the group said, expenditures for foreign students would come to at least $3,540,000. Since foreign students tend to be concentrated in the higher-cost upper division and graduate school, however, it calculated the cost was "probably as much as $4,500,000." Some of this was recaptured through federal and other funds, but in the end $1,000,000 had to be made up largely through state appropriations—and even this did not count amortization on buildings and equipment.

The group did not claim that California figures are typical of publicly supported universities—"Over the country they may be on the high side." Nevertheless, it contended:

The difference between the amount expended by the publicly supported universities on federally sponsored foreign students and the fee income received from the federal government for such students is very substantial. This should not be. The states should not be called upon to subsidize the federal government for the education of federally sponsored foreign students.

Rather, the federal government should pay the full cost of educating such students, including a fair allowance for capital outlay.

Summarizing, the group estimated on a national basis that cost of instruction and capital outlay by universities, and living and travel costs of foreign students, would "at midpoint" come to $5,400 per student per year. Thus the cost to the federal government to sponsor the recommended 20,000-odd foreign students would be $108 million per year.

CHAPTER SEVEN

Education of Americans for Service Overseas

In Chapter 4 it was explained that the findings of International Study Group III fell logically into two parts, the first dealing with the creation in the American people of an awareness and understanding of international affairs and the second with on-campus education of Americans to serve abroad.

Chapter 4 took up the work of Land-Grant colleges and universities in connection with the first area as well as the broad findings of Group IV, relating to the responsibilities of state and federal governments for international educational activities in general. This chapter will discuss Group III's report on education of Americans for service abroad, together with that part of Group IV's report covering the financing of this activity.

" 'Education applied to the needs of life,' " to repeat a brief extract from Group III's report, quoted in Chapter 4, "has been a distinctive contribution of the Land-Grant colleges in the past 100 years. This concept is being increasingly accepted by all education. The time has come for the Land-Grant colleges to work with all forces of education to build a world in which all human beings can survive and thrive. The Land-Grant colleges, by their philosophy, experience, and organization, are uniquely equipped to assist in this task."

Agreeing completely with this statement of position,

Group IV voiced this blunt opinion: "Unquestionably, resident instruction for U.S. nationals in both international affairs (for foreign service) and international studies (for U.S. citizens working and living at home) needs improvement, expansion and intensification."

Some evidence of the direction in which we should move, Group IV said, is found in study of degrees conferred by U.S. universities and colleges. In the 1959-60 academic year, the latest report by the U.S. Office of Education, some 394,889 bachelor's degrees were awarded by all U.S. institutions of higher learning. Of these, only 5,498 were in foreign languages and literature, including linguistics. Moreover, only six were in Chinese, four in Japanese, and 102 in Russian.

"It is certainly evident," Group IV observed, "that American higher education is almost exclusively oriented toward the European languages," to the neglect of the many Asiatic, African, and Middle Eastern tongues which are becoming so increasingly important.

In social science fields which have a particular bearing on world affairs—anthropology, political science, and the like—degrees were similarly scattered.

Discouraging as this may appear, it can at least be said that the Land-Grant institutions, which enroll about 20 per cent of all U.S. college-level students, carried their share of the load as a group, in all these subjects. The following tabulation shows number of B.A. degrees granted by Land-Grant institutions and the percentage of the whole represented by the Land-Grant figures:

Field	All U.S. Institutions	Land-Grant Institutions	Per Cent of Land-Grant Graduates to Total
	Number of Graduates 1959-60		
Chinese	6	0	0.0
Japanese	4	4	100.0

Field	Number of Graduates 1959-60		Per Cent of Land-Grant Graduates to Total
	All U.S. Institutions	Land-Grant Institutions	
Russian	102	22	21.6
Anthropology	413	122	29.5
Area and regional studies	268	80	29.9
International relations	447	56	12.5
Foreign Service programs	142	21	14.8
Political science and government	6,657	1,502	22.6
Sociology	7,182	1,088	15.1

Another index to Land-Grant participation in international studies is the fact that 17 out of 54 "Language and Area Centers" set up under the 1958 National Defense Education Act, or about 30 per cent, are located at Land-Grant institutions. These centers, almost all of which are at the graduate level, offer study primarily in the "neglected" languages of Asia, Africa, and the Middle East, and—just as important—in the culture, economics, and so on of the areas in which these languages are spoken. The centers located on Land-Grant campuses are:

University of Arizona: Oriental; Latin American.

University of California, Berkeley: South Asian; East European.

University of California, Los Angeles: African; Latin American; Near Eastern.

Cornell University: South Asian; Southeast Asian; East Asian.

University of Florida: Latin American.

University of Hawaii: Chinese, Japanese, and Korean; Indonesian, Javanese, and Thai.

University of Illinois: Russian.

Michigan State University: African.

University of Wisconsin: South Asian; Latin American.

None of these centers came into existence as such, with federal support, prior to 1959, the year after passage of the

Defense Education Act, which also promotes language study through fellowships in the "neglected" languages, through summer and academic year institutes for high school language teachers and through research in language and linguistics.

This does not mean, however, that Land-Grant and other universities and colleges had not been active in international affairs before 1958. Many had; in fact, in some cases an activity of long standing was converted almost bodily into one of the new centers. On the other hand, some previously active programs in language or area work, or both, have continued as they were, not seeking federal support. Among the latter are two at Land-Grant institutions which Group III pinpointed as doing particularly effective work, at Montana State College and Texas Agricultural and Mechanical College.

The International Cooperation Center at Montana State College was established in 1956 after months of studying the most effective ways of relating the college to programs of international education and technical cooperation. The responsibilities and interest of the center are campuswide. These include administration of the college's technical cooperation contracts with the U.S. government and other agencies abroad; recruitment and orientation of Americans for technical service overseas; cooperation with those responsible for the work with foreign students and International Farm Youth Exchange programs; and assistance in seminars and conferences related to international understanding.

In 1958, an experimental graduate study program was designed to train Americans for technical service abroad under a grant from the Carnegie Corporation. This program, for students who are mature and experienced enough to be reasonably certain of their career interests, provides for advanced study leading to a master's degree in agriculture, engineering, education, health education, or home economics.

The two-year course of instruction is in three parts: (1) the courses in the technical (major) field, as determined by the departments concerned, to meet degree requirements; (2) the cross-cultural communications component, taken by all students regardless of technical field, which includes courses and seminars in world geography, world cultures, process of economic development, American diplomatic history and language, etc.; (3) field projects in the United States and abroad, which place all students in situations demanding cultural understanding, and also enable each student to use his technical skill in projects of agricultural improvement, public health, and community development.

Since the wives of married students are a very important factor in overseas adjustment, they participate in seminars, language courses, and field projects.

The Texas A & M program, supported by the Ford Foundation, is to prepare professors for service in A & M's own AID project in East Pakistan, where it works with the University of Dacca in education, business administration, agriculture, and home economics.

"One of the serious problems which these [Land-Grant] institutions face," Group III reported in appraising some of the difficulties of overseas activity, "has been the selection and training of their own professors for service in their foreign projects. . . . Since operating funds are limited, periods of orientation and training have necessarily been short."

The problem which Texas A & M set out to solve was how to make the best use of this short time. Its solution was to give a professor a 30-day intensive course on the campus before sending him to East Pakistan, where he receives further in-service training.

Campus training includes families for the study of language and the problems of adjusting to the culture of the host country. The content of the training is as follows:

1. *The Bengali language.* In 30 days, 90 hours of intensive

instruction is given in speaking and understanding Bengali. This instruction utilizes a trained linguist, a native speaker, and a language laboratory with tapes especially prepared for the purpose. This intensive training is designed to form a foundation upon which a staff member can build after he reaches East Pakistan. The follow-up of this intensive period of training includes the supplying of Bengali tapes to the family after it reaches Pakistan for use in further study and drill, and periodic checking of progress.

2. *The problems of adjusting to and living in East Pakistan.* Twenty hours of instruction and discussion are devoted to such basic concepts as culture, value systems, etc. Use is made of round-table discussions, utilizing families with experience in foreign service and Pakistan staff on the campus as resource people. Problems of health, servant troubles, food, clothes, entertainment of Pakistani hosts, special customs, etc., consume most of the time.

3. *Problems encountered in bringing about desired changes in the host institution.* Twenty hours of instruction and discussion are conducted on this subject, using actual problems as the basis for discussion.

4. *The problems of economic development of underdeveloped countries, with special reference to Pakistan.* Twenty hours are devoted to this subject. The Pakistan plan for economic and social development is discussed and the role of Texas A & M's host institutions in this plan is explained.

A secondary aim of this program of training is to establish regular course offerings in the fields considered crucial in preparing technical assistance agents for overseas service. Three such courses have been established: (1) applied anthropology, a course based upon the problems American families encounter in living and working in a foreign culture in newly developing countries; (2) the methods of planning technological changes and putting them into effect; (3) the problems of economic development in newly developing countries.

Each of these three courses is designed for graduate and advanced undergraduate students of agriculture, engineering, or veterinary science, with no social science prerequisites required except those normally taken by students from these fields.

"The fact that scores of Texas A & M graduates are serving in foreign technical programs," Group III declared, "and that the current crop of students is displaying more and more interest in going into such programs, seems to point up the need for such courses."

Activity of a slightly different sort, springing from the critical need for agricultural workers in developing nations, is a kind of program in operation at several Land-Grant institutions, in which people are trained specifically for overseas work in agriculture.

Among the institutions conducting programs of this sort is Iowa State University, which was one of the first to be asked to set up a Peace Corps training center. It trained 15 agricultural workers for St. Lucia in the British West Indies.

With their recognized tradition of doing just the kind of work with people which the Corps is called upon to perform, six of the first 10 universities asked to assist in Peace Corps training in 1961 were Land-Grant. Aside from Iowa State, they were: the Berkeley campus of the University of California, which trained 51 secondary and university teachers bound for Ghana; California's Los Angeles campus, which trained 45 persons in the same fields for service in Nigeria; Colorado State, 28 agricultural extension, health, and education workers for West Pakistan; Rutgers (New Jersey), 62 community development experts for Colombia; The Ohio State University, 26 agricultural workers for India.

At work in 1962 were these Land-Grant universities: New Mexico State, 25 agricultural extension workers for El Salvador; Pennsylvania State, 42 educational workers for Ceylon; University of Puerto Rico, 21 agricultural extension workers for the Dominican Republic.

A misgiving that Group III expressed about these courses was that they were too short and intensive, few of them lasting much more than a month or two.

It may be that the Peace Corps orientation and training programs attempt to do too much in too little time. When compared with other specialized programs, the training programs developed to date appear to move at a very fast pace, with heavy reliance on lectures and other materials to which the volunteers are exposed.

Some educators question whether this sort of training, with the "trainer" or professor calling the signals, will equip Peace Corps volunteers to function in a real life situation which demands that they must have initiative, exercise judgment and establish relationships. Perhaps a program making provision for more deliberation, reflection, problem solving, adaptation, and evaluation would utilize the resources within the volunteers and make more serious demands upon the individual, thus inducing more growth of the qualities needed in overseas work.

(Since the Group III report was issued, the Peace Corps has extended the time of its training programs to a minimum of three months in most cases, with much greater emphasis on languages. Depending on the nature of the project and the difficulty of the language, from a third to a half of the training period is devoted to language.)

Group III made clear that in its view every training program for overseas service in existence today is still in the experimental stage—"In none of them has there been sufficient time or experience to do more than identify problems and point directions." It even raised the question whether people of college age are "trainable" at all for overseas work since their attitudes are already pretty well set. The best method of bringing people into this field, it suggested, may be simply to select those whose personalities and views toward other peoples mark them as likely to succeed.

In any case, Group III concluded, "experience of those

who have experimented with such programs indicates the following requirements": (1) well-developed academic departments to provide both technical and cultural training for work abroad; (2) a permanent field laboratory or work project or contact with a university operating in the area (or areas) of assignment with facilities and staff for in-service training and counseling; (3) some system, at the undergraduate level, which would facilitate search for talent and provide opportunity for voluntary experiences of an increasing level of involvement and responsibility; (4) some system whereby graduates can make contact with possible employers and secure work which would utilize their technical skill and international understanding; (5) a service of guided professional growth for those who have done well in initial overseas assignment and wish to make international work a career; (6) a built-in means of continuous evaluation and redirection.

To Study Group IV, assessing the responsibility for support of instruction of U.S. nationals for service abroad, two possible viewpoints suggested themselves: "One attitude would accept the premise that federal support for resident instruction, research and extension should be the same for international studies as for any other programs.

"The other position is that special consideration should be given to preparation of students for careers abroad, since the U.S. government has a direct concern with how well these emissaries, official and otherwise, have been prepared for foreign service."

For itself, Study Group IV took this position:

Revision and expansion of international studies of benefit to Americans who are not oriented toward foreign service should be borne by the states.

However, modest federal support, along the lines of the Morrill Act, will serve to stimulate resident instruction for citizens who will work in the international field. Federal funds should be apportioned to the states in proportion to enrollment in public higher education. Federal funds should be provided for scholarships and faculty fellowships for U.S. nationals studying international affairs in foreign countries. . . .

Admittedly it is difficult to differentiate between studies for Americans serving international fields and those who stay at home. However, enlargment of language and area studies, under federal sponsorship, for Americans oriented toward international service careers will surely stimulate added interest and activity for other students and assist the universities and colleges to enlarge international studies for all Americans.

The magnitude of federal support of studies for international service should be a subject of further study.

Group IV also discussed the need for an enormous amount of research into such areas as the personal characteristics desirable in persons going overseas, the actual needs (rather than politically expedient needs) of countries receiving assistance, the ways American methods and techniques can be best adapted to foreign situations, and —with an eye to revising them in the light of experience— the effectiveness of U.S. programs abroad.

"Research should receive increased support," it said, "in at least the following measures" (in general, shared responsibility between federal and state governments):

The federal government should assume responsibility for financing, via the mechanism of the institutional grant, a number of strong research centers in international affairs. Such centers would be dedicated to the study of international affairs in the broad sense of sponsoring investigations into the social, economic, geographic, and cultural aspects of given areas of the world. In their investigations they would call upon the services of scholars from the sciences, the social sciences, and the humanities.

It is expected that concentration on a selected geographical area will be conducted on a multidisciplinary level; such research will require stronger library facilities. Several international studies centers have made a good start and offer highly promising models of how such ventures are established and conducted.

Federal funds should also be channeled to underwrite a substantial program of faculty research grants to competent and qualified individuals in any public university on the basis of approved projects on international matters.

The flow of federal funds to develop research centers and faculty research should be accompanied by increasing state support, in step with rising residence instruction, for departmental research for normal professional advancement, thus helping to preserve state and federal support that has traditionally distinguished the Land-Grant universities and colleges.

To create a mechanism for providing federal funds, individual or institutional, and to avoid duplication, a pattern should be established for allocation of such funds. A pattern analogous to those of the National Science Foundation and the U.S. Public Health Service might be used.

The National Science Foundation, in a pamphlet titled "Program Activities," describes its research grant pattern in these words: "Ordinarily, proposals are initiated by an individual scientist and submitted by the institution with which he is affiliated. In order to be considered by the Foundation, such a proposal must carry the endorsement of the institution."

The pamphlet also points out that by executive order "the Foundation is instructed to recommend to the President 'policies for the promotion and support of basic research and education in the sciences, including policies with respect to furnishing guidance toward defining the responsibilities of the federal government in the conduct and support of basic scientific research.'"

In calling for heavy federal support of research in international education "similar to support given to research in agriculture, health and space-age and atomic-age problems," Group IV rested its case on a single basic proposition: the government is the only agency that can carry the load. "The universities are powerful," it said, "but without support they cannot do their best, and nothing but their best is good enough."

CHAPTER EIGHT

Recommendations on International Affairs

Each of the four international study groups concluded its report with recommendations for action. Inevitably, there was some overlapping and partial duplication, and so after the Kansas City Convocation the four chairmen decided to consolidate all recommendations into a single cohesive document. This document subsequently was adopted by the Senate of the Land-Grant association, its governing body of presidents and deans, as an official statement of position.

The reworked recommendations fell into three categories: to the Association of State Universities and Land-Grant Colleges as a body; to the Land-Grant institutions as individual colleges and universities; and to U.S. government agencies concerned with international education.

Those recommendations addressed to the Association dealt with internal procedural matters of no general interest except for one which proposed that continuing study committees be named to work with the Association's standing International Affairs Committee. Following are the recommendations in the second and third categories.

II. To LAND-GRANT COLLEGES AND UNIVERSITIES—*To improve and strengthen programs in international education, the Centennial International Study Groups suggest that the colleges and universities:*

A. Examine the possibilities of improving their educational programs in developing countries by taking the following steps:

1. Prior to involvement in a government or foundation-sponsored grant or contract overseas, the university should institute careful study in the host country and on its campus to determine:

   a. Whether the proposed program is one which meets genuine needs of the people in the host country in their social, economic, and political context;

   b. Whether the potential for change within the host country gives promise of a successful program;

   c. Whether the program is feasible for the university to undertake in terms of its resources—faculty, administrative personnel, and areas of specialization required;

   d. Whether active cooperation on the part of the host country may be reasonably expected in planning, developing, and sustaining the program;

   e. Whether the university is willing and able to conduct departmental research activities to undergird the program.

2. After careful appraisal has been made and the decision reached to proceed with a project abroad, the university (with due regard for decisions and policies established by our government) should take responsibility for developing a well-planned program in cooperation with the sponsoring agency and responsible people in the host country. It should avoid mere adoption, without critical study, of a project proposed by government or a foundation.

3. Overseas programs should become an *integral* part of the university, or a major division thereof, with deep commitment on the part of faculty and administration.

4. The university should improve its internal organ-

ization to take maximum advantage of the opportunities offered by programs overseas and provide incentives for participation by qualified staff members by:

  a. Protection of tenure and promotion of rights;
  b. Better selection and orientation of staff members and families for overseas living and working;
  c. Adequate financial support to meet the added expense of overseas travel and living.

5. Long-range plans should be based on a continuing appraisal of the university's efforts overseas by people in the host country, in the United States Government, at the university, and by objective "outsiders."

6. Care should be taken to avoid overextension, to consolidate experience gained in each international project, and to coordinate work conducted in several countries.

7. Insofar as practical and appropriate, a priority for U.S. universities in developing countries should be to strengthen and develop educational institutions within the host country.

B. Strengthen programs on campus for (1) foreign scholars, students, and trainees, and (2) American students and the citizenry in general, by:

1. In programs for foreign scholars, students, and trainees:

  a. Providing high-quality educational opportunities, including work experience where appropriate and feasible, adapted to the needs of foreign students, which does not necessarily mean offering identical curricula to that offered other students, but rather offering a type of "honors course" to utilize the foreign student's background and to give him appropriate courses for his needs;

  b. Providing special seminars in such subjects as educational methods, social psychology (as related to technological change), and public administration to facilitate effective use of knowledge and skill of the foreign student on return to his homeland;

c. Providing trained and adequate staff to ensure visiting foreign students and specialists of hospitality, convenient accommodations, and effective counseling (which should not preclude efforts to integrate foreign students into normal counseling, extracurricular activities, and student programs);

d. Providing opportunities for foreign students and specialists to study the Land-Grant institution's services to the state;

e. Emphasizing among faculty and students the fact that there is no substitute for personal interest in foreign students. Adequate finances, suitable accommodations, assistance in locating summer employment, and well-conceived curricula, though vitally important, cannot succeed in the absence of a courteous, friendly atmosphere.

2. In programs to prepare Americans to serve abroad and to build awareness among the citizenry of this country's role in world affairs:

a. Making more effective use of foreign students to enrich the intellectual life of the campus (foreign visitors can contribute to creating a more realistic and vivid understanding of other cultures and problems in international affairs);

b. Strengthening the curriculum by:
   (1) Offering courses for undergraduates in non-Western civilizations and cultural anthropology,
   (2) Adding international perspective to appropriate on-going courses;

c. Establishing a center with campuswide relationships to:
   (1) Gather information from agencies and organizations involved in world affairs and to make this available to the campus, community, and state,

    (2) Serve as stimulus for extracurricular international activities on and off campus,

    (3) Serve as a channel of information about overseas assignments and work of the university in overseas programs,

    (4) Work closely with those responsible for international students—to strengthen this program and utilize it in enrichment of campus and curricular life;

  d. Developing a system to utilize cooperative and general extension for world affairs education;

  e. Seeking state support for international cultural studies for adults.

III. To U.S. Government Agencies Involved in International Education Programs with Land-Grant Colleges and Universities—*To support the universities in their efforts to improve the quality and enlarge the scope of international educational programs, much larger sums of money will be needed. As in the past, private sources and state governments will supply an important part of the funds required, but the assistance of the federal government is also needed. The Association of State Universities and Land-Grant Colleges suggests:*

A. That there be a substantial expansion of expenditures (50 per cent at least, initially) to support U.S. government-sponsored foreign undergraduate and graduate students and faculty and their families in the United States.[1]

B. That a much larger number of qualified students and faculty members, particularly from the developing nations, be given opportunities to study in the United States, with the proviso that numbers be subordinated to the selection of high-quality students and the continuation of a high-quality educational program.

[1] Possible costs are estimated as follows: instruction and capital outlay, $1,500 to $2,500 per student per year; living costs, $2,000 to $3,000 per student per year; travel to and from the United States, $300 to $1,500 per student.

C. That the federal government subsidize all costs for participating institutions in contractual arrangements, including capital outlay, and living and travel expenses for foreigners.

D. That substantial federal financing is needed to assist institutions in providing a number of services, particularly a foreign student advisory office to enable them to provide genuine counseling services, special educational programs, and a variety of activities which could lead to better campus programs, supervision, reports, and evaluation.

E. That a substantial increase in funds be made available for supporting procedures overseas for the proper selection and placement of foreign students in U.S. colleges and universities, [2] including:

 1. Strengthening of U.S. educational commissions abroad by providing an adequate number of professional staff members for counseling and selection;

 2. Provision of better guidance to educational commissions regarding utilization of appropriate colleges and universities throughout the United States (a wider distribution of foreign students among qualified institutions is needed, and more effective use should be made of technical institutes, community colleges, and small four-year colleges than at present);

 3. Establishment of English-language instruction centers overseas and in the United States for all foreign students and trainees needing instruction;

 4. Orientation programs for all students before departure from their homeland, upon arrival in the United States, and before departure from the United States.

F. That the federal agencies sponsoring foreign educational projects consult with prospective contracting universities at the earliest possible stage so that they may participate in development of the project.

[2] The Mutual Educational and Cultural Exchange Act of 1961 permits federal agencies to support many of the activities proposed.

G. That assistance programs to foreign universities should be substantially expanded on a long-term basis, with all costs borne by the federal government and responsibility for shaping the program placed in the hands of the contracting U.S. college or university.

H. That assistance be given to the states to expand studies and training for students preparing for international service.

I. That federal grants similar to those made by the National Science Foundation and the Department of Health, Education, and Welfare be awarded for university-centered research in international affairs to:

 1. Provide continuing assessment of overseas educational programs;

 2. Determine the impact of U.S. university experience on foreign students and specialists and their contribution to their national life—and the impact of foreign students and specialists on the host university and community life;

 3. Evaluate short-term training as a contribution to social and economic advancement in newly developing countries;

 4. Appraise the role of short-term training as an instrument of U.S. foreign policy.

J. That adult education of U.S. nationals in international studies be expanded. (While this is principally the responsibility of the states, there appears to be no alternative to federal aid if the job is to be done. The general extension proposal considered by the Eighty-seventh Congress should be pressed in the next session, particularly because of its potential in world affairs education for adults.)

K. That experimentation should continue in the use of third-country training.

PART TWO

Improving Education

_____

"How, it was once asked, can you deal with large numbers and provide quality education? Be professionally motivated and liberally educated? . . . The answer comes back, boldly and clearly, that we are doing both and will continue to do both." The words are those of President David D. Henry of the University of Illinois, who cautioned, nevertheless, in his speech at Kansas City, that "in some areas even our best is not good enough." Part Two of this volume tells how Land-Grant institutions stand educationally after a century of life and what they are doing to strengthen their efforts for the next century.

CHAPTER NINE

Liberal Arts and Humanities

". . . the leading object shall be, *without excluding other scientific and classical studies* and including military tactics, to teach such branches of learning as are related to agriculture and the mechanic arts. . . ."

To Justin Smith Morrill, the italicized words in this passage from the act which he fought through Congress meant all that they said, and more. It was his frequently expressed intention that, far from merely *not excluding* these studies, the Land-Grant colleges endowed under the act should in a positive and aggressive way *include* them in their curricula.

What Morrill called scientific and classical studies are what we know today as "the liberal arts" or "the arts and sciences." They include the humanities—language, literature, and the fine arts—the natural sciences, and the social sciences, with one important stipulation, which is that in the sense that they are "liberal" they are not taught as vocations. That is to say, although many a young American may eventually become a professional in one of these fields, when he takes biology or economics in a college of arts and sciences he does not do so to learn how to be a biologist or economist but simply to gain an appreciation of biology and economics as part of the world in which he lives.

That such an appreciation, in a world growing daily more confusing, is essential for constructive citizenship is a fact not wasted on the thoughtful leaders of our Land-

Grant system. Even in such fields as agriculture and engineering, in which at one time it was widely accepted that technical training was all that was necessary, there is a growing demand for liberal education. What is being done in these two areas in particular will be detailed in the later chapters covering them.

The views of such a man as Glenn T. Seaborg, former chancellor of the Berkeley campus of the University of California and now chairman of the U.S. Atomic Energy Commission—that "the long war of the mind will be won in the classroom, in the libraries, and in the laboratories"— have already been cited.

Seaborg's words were amplified at Kansas City by another man intimately familiar with the demands for educated brainpower in today's world, President John A. Perkins of the University of Delaware, who as president of the Land-Grant association said in his keynote speech:

Academic specialization will doubtless be carried to still greater lengths now that technological and scientific knowledge have come to count for more than military and administrative skill in the area of international power politics. This necessity to specialize must be accompanied by a renewed emphasis upon the liberal arts or we will defeat our own purposes.

There are at least two reasons: The pursuit of natural science can become sterile if it is cut off from the comprehensive and philosophical thought from which it sprang; further, important as has been our contribution in the natural sciences and the mechanic arts, if we are to remain a free society, there is a mandate upon us not to neglect the classical and liberal studies. The importance of these studies is that they not only cultivate brains but are especially capable of producing the better character requisite for self-governing citizens.

In our time, enlightened and devoted citizenship is *the* practical vocation of life. To say as much is not to excuse for a moment other departments and schools in our universities from doing their part in this essential task of inculcating the needed qualities of steadfast character. It nevertheless is the special responsibility of those departments which have evolved from the classics and moral philosophy. Character is needed if big democracy is not to degenerate into group selfishness.

Today more than a third of the undergraduate students at Land-Grant institutions are enrolled in these institutions' colleges of arts and sciences, and this does not count the thousands of students enrolled in professional schools—engineering, agriculture, teacher education, and the like—who are required to take perhaps as much as half their work in liberal arts. It would be almost impossibly difficult to calculate the number of such students, or the proportion of their academic programs devoted to liberal arts, but it is a fair guess that every one of the some 425,000 full-time undergraduates in Land-Grant institutions enjoys some exposure to them.

Numbers of students, of course, is one thing. The quality of the courses offered to them is another. Consistent with the nagging self-examination to which conscientious educators are constantly subjecting themselves, it was with deep interest that the Land-Grant deans of arts and sciences listened to the words of George D. Stoddard, former president of the Land-Grant University of Illinois, now chancellor of New York University, a private institution, who acted as outside evaluator in this field at Kansas City.

Stoddard, in a remarkably lucid paper, first set out a definition for liberal arts, then examined how the teaching in Land-Grant institutions meets these tests, and finally presented some concrete recommendations.

In reply to his own question, "What is meant by the liberal arts?" Stoddard listed four points of definition:

1. The subject matter is enduring . . . a search for abstract principles, generative ideas and art forms—for all that gives meaning and value to life. "How-to-do-it" courses cannot meet this test.

2. The subject matter is whole. . . . However brief the course, it will start with questions . . . may end with more questions, and perhaps with a few answers, but it will require the student to think for himself.

3. The student approaches the subject matter without reference to technical application. . . . It should not take him long to discover that he is achieving a new literacy, as it were, that will brighten his life on many occasions and in all cultures.

4. Liberal education is a common language . . . that all persons may employ apart from "shop talk." Technical fields should contribute richly to this pool of communicable knowledge [but] there must be some principle of selection for the non-specialist. . . . Liberal education is a form of intellectual currency that can be acquired to some degree by every student.

Not everything in even the best liberal arts colleges, Stoddard made clear, can be regarded altogether as liberal education. The difference comes in the subjects which are required by a student's "major." These Stoddard referred to as "specialized" subjects.

"There is no clear-cut dividing line," Stoddard conceded. "All required courses comprising a 'major' in arts and sciences are regarded as specialized; 'elective' courses may or may not be. Thus, for a physics major, mathematics is considered to be a part of the student's specialized education." On the other hand, if an English major took mathematics, just for the joy of it, it would be considered truly liberal.

"At the risk of oversimplification," Stoddard summed up before proceeding to his appraisal of the work of Land-Grant arts colleges, "I should say that the keynote in liberal education is allurement, and the keynote in specialization is commitment. The one facilitates communication and broadens the learning experience; the other carries a vocational or professional implication."

In a nutshell, Stoddard's analysis of the effectiveness of Land-Grant teaching in the arts and sciences can be put in his own words thus: "It makes an enormous difference to a talented student what state he happens to reside in; the range of educational opportunity is from the niggardly to the magnificent. . . . Apart from vocationally oriented work in agriculture, engineering and teacher training, some Land-Grant institutions have not evolved with the times; they are meager. . . . Quality has often been sacrificed, especially in the small separated Land-Grant universities of the more impoverished states."

Stoddard conceded that "there is, of course, room for

difference." However, he quickly added, "I am referring to *quality* and to a *diversity of program* that satisfies the many-faceted talent of youth and the demand for expertise in the 20th century life of the American people." As examples of magnificent or near-magnificent educational opportunities, Stoddard cited:

In the natural sciences, the University of California, which offers work leading to the B.A. degree in astronomy, bacteriology, botany, chemistry, geology, mathematics, meteorology, physics, and zoology, and supports interdepartmental concentrations in astronomy-physics, biological illustration, biophysics, earth physics, geophysics, and physical sciences–mathematics.

In the social sciences, the University of Kentucky, with courses in anthropology, archeology, commerce, economics, education, geography, history, law, philosophy, political science, psychology, social work, and sociology.

In the fine arts, Florida Agricultural and Mechanical University, where a four-year course in that field includes English, world civilization, mathematics, a foreign language, world literature, biology, physical science, psychology, and social science, as well as fine arts work in such areas as drawing, sculpture, water color, metal and wood design, pottery, textiles, and mural painting.

In languages, the University of Wisconsin, which offers Arabic, Chinese, French, German, Greek, Hebrew, Hindi and Telegu (both spoken in India), Italian, Latin, Polish, Portuguese, Russian, Sanskrit (the ancient language of India), Scandinavian languages, and Spanish. "Other Land-Grant universities," Stoddard commented, "considering what they *could* offer, might ponder the Wisconsin list."

With reference to the offerings of all four universities, he declared: "If these universities are justified in offering what they do offer at public expense—and I believe the evidence is overwhelming—we can at least ask a state or Land-Grant institution for a clear defense of its policy in offering something less."

In addition to course offerings, Stoddard examined three other points as indicative of the standards of the Land-Grant universities and colleges. These were "general education" programs, "honors" programs, and libraries.

Many of the larger universities require all undergraduate students to take a basic or "general education" program in liberal arts and sciences. One such which has gained wide favorable attention is the Basic College at Michigan State University. Every MSU undergraduate is required to take 45 term-credits in this college in "communication skills" (English), natural science, social science, and the humanities, regardless of his major field. He may speed up these studies by passing comprehensive examinations in them.

As another "outstanding exception" to his general statement that "at times these sequences do not seem to be highly organized," Stoddard cited the plan at the University of Minnesota. Here a two-year junior college offers work in 26 departments. A student may stop with two years, taking an associate in arts degree, or he may continue for two more years in the College of Science, Literature and the Arts, of which the junior college is a part, and earn his bachelor's degree.

Stoddard noted also that Minnesota's Division of General Studies makes it possible for students to take interdepartmental work, supplementing the work of the various individual departments, in six groups of courses: "communications" (English), family life (nutrition, child development, etc.), humanities, natural science, personal orientation, and social science. Continuing, he said:

> While many universities, through electives, would permit students to take work in such areas, it is likely that few do so in the absence of a definite plan. Also the work often needs a different approach from that found in technical sequences.
>
> Thus, in this context, I would agree that academic work in nutrition, consumer education and child development, more often than not avoided by curriculum designers in the arts and sciences, would be more appropriate than slight additions to a long scholastic sequence in the language arts. In our culture

pattern, which is strongly affected by fads, fashions and commercial pressures, an objective collegiate program on family life takes on the status of an imperative.

The Land-Grant universities, while in advance of others in this respect, have not as yet fully placed such work within the scope of a liberal education for all students.

"Honors" work consists of programs for gifted and highly motivated students who are freed for a few hours each week from routine classes to pursue work of their own choosing in library or laboratory. Their contact with faculty members is generally in small seminars or individual conferences. Participation in these courses is considered a privilege and admission to them is limited.

Stoddard picked no quarrel with the aims of honors work as found in most Land-Grant universities, but he did report that honors plans as he found them in his study "leave me with an uneasy feeling that they more often proclaim virtues than attain them."

"An institution addicted to 'routine teaching' at any level of student talent," he said, without naming any institution so addicted,

is likely also to develop a program of routine examinations and a routine supervision of individualized instruction. Similarly, deficiencies in library and laboratory facilities are not removed by the simple expedient of permitting bright students to be left to their own resources. . . . Better than most honors programs are the programs of high intensity in science, foreign languages, public affairs and the creative arts. For the most part, these developments, often interdepartmental, escape the pious approach that is the occupational hazard of all plans for honors and independent study.

Actually, Stoddard saw both honors and high-intensity programs as manifestations of what he called "a search for ways to end the fragmentation that has grown like a virus in our higher education system." He commented:

Students in their general approach are observers and inheritors. Only through intense application will they themselves discover the travail that accompanies new insight. The general approach is defensible if it sets real problems and, above all, leads the student to specialize in at least one field of knowledge. This is the reason for requiring a major within the four-year liberal arts curriculum—a major that, in my opinion, should dig more deeply than those found today in the Land-Grant university college of arts and sciences.

It would be profitable if every Land-Grant institution would analyze its offerings for all levels of student ability and achievement. The lowliest bona fide students are as typical of a university as the more talked about top ten percent. Average students are still more numerous. What is being done about them? The answer is so vague as to arouse suspicion. Such students are rarely mentioned!

As with course offerings, so with libraries, as Stoddard reported on them after analyzing catalog descriptions. There was a tremendous range, he said, in this case "from the shamefully deficient to the magnificent," and he added:

> Some catalogs devote numerous pages to acreage, admissions, dining and housing facilities . . . but neglect to say one word about the resources in books, documents and journals. Surely there is a relationship between this neglect and a low library status.
>
> On the other hand, there are bright spots: Minnesota (2,-000,000 items), Wisconsin (over 2,000,000 items), California (several million items), Washington State University (2,000,-000 items). Of all these places, the brightest is the University of Illinois. . . . Its present collections exceed 3,383,000 volumes, and all except about 245,000 of them are located in Urbana [the rest are at the university's two Chicago campuses].
>
> Thus we have in the isolated community of Urbana-Champaign, the seat of a Land-Grant university that opened its doors in 1868, a library surpassed in the United States only by the Harvard library and the Library of Congress.

No one, Stoddard conceded, "expects many universities to catch up with Harvard, Illinois or Yale in all-'round excellence." Nevertheless, he added, "that does not excuse a penny-pinching attitude on the part of states and boards of trustees" where it exists with respect to libraries.

Stoddard concluded his paper by sketching "A New Approach to Education in the Land-Grant Universities."

"I am not interested in just shoring up the curricula of colleges and universities," he said. "My concern is not with the minutiae of academic progress. . . . The superior Land-Grant universities, by first emphasizing science and lately the fine arts, have given new weight to the contemporary idea of a complete education. If they will now develop curricula that combine intensive specialization and unfragmented liberal studies, while wholeheartedly advancing the art of teaching, they may again move forward as pioneers."

The "new approach" which Stoddard presented was an effort to set out just such a curriculum. It is presented here slightly abridged:

The price to be paid for excellence is clear. It calls for a limited program of subjects for a given student, the student to study each subject intensively over a long period of time. This means that college education should be based squarely on a double standard—one standard for the *cultural imperatives* and a different one for the *cultural electives*. By "cultural imperatives" I mean the English language and the social studies (including science appreciation and art appreciation), together with a cluster of common skills and experiences. By "cultural electives" I mean science, art (performance), and foreign languages. A student's major specialization is, of course, independent of this duality.

As a base, subject to modification in response to the aims, purposes, and choices of a particular Land-Grant university, I suggest the following diagrammatic approach to a curriculum in the liberal arts and sciences:

Arts and Sciences
Semester Hours (for the baccalaureate, 128 hours)°

	Year I	Year II	Year III	Year IV	Total
A. General education					
(a) Cultural imperatives	10	8	8	6	32
(b) Cultural electives	10	8	8	6	32
B. Specialization (the major-minor sequences)	12	16	16	20	64
Year totals	32	32	32	32	128

° To be pro-rated for quarter-hours or differences in the number of hours required for the degree.

This scheme differs from what is found in most Land-Grant universities in three respects:

1. The allowance of 64 hours, the equivalent of two years, for specialization (a major-minor sequence). Generally a university permits majors to account for not more than 40 hours credit, and they may run as low as 24 hours. A related minor is often allotted less than one-half the hours required for a major. Hence this plan offers more study *in depth.*

2. The major-minor companionship is replaced by the single term, *specialization.* It may be contained in a single department, divided between two departments, or spread over several as in "area" studies.

3. A new duality is introduced—that between *cultural imperatives* and *cultural electives*—with correlated differences in the organization of subject matter and methods of teaching. . . .

Very well perhaps in theory, but how can such a scheme be adapted to what is actually found, or could be found, in our Land-Grant universities? This is not the place to spell out details, but an example may be submitted.

The *cultural imperatives* are found in the programs of every college or school of the arts and sciences. (They are not thus far available in just this sequence of 10, 8, 8, and 6 semester hours, constituting the equivalent of a full year of undergraduate study.) However, English, the social studies, and art appreciation are often found in programs of general education available to every student. The common practice is that students specializing in a field need not take the required general courses in that field, although as freshmen they may find some of the courses quite appropriate. English covers speech, writing, literature, and philology. The social studies cover history, government (political science), economics, anthropology, psychology, sociology, philosophy, and international affairs.

Similarly, the cultural electives could be organized into the equivalent of a year's academic experience on a moderately descending scale over the four years. A choice among three streams is suggested:

1. Natural science—a coordinated program in mathematics, physics, chemistry, earth sciences, biology, and astronomy, or

2. Foreign language—one or two languages, of which one is preferably a continuation of two or more years of the language in high school, together with correlated "area" studies, or

3. The visual or performing arts—a program combining theoretical and practical work in such fields as drawing, painting, sculpture, music, the theater arts.

Specializations are almost "too numerous to mention." Ideally each university should restrict them to subjects, fields, or areas that it can fully support through staff, facilities, and an intensive curricular offering. For many students the specialization will be the beginning of advanced work as a graduate or professional student. In this 64-hour segment the emphasis is on intensity and continuity. The student is free to choose a specialty within the offerings of a particular university (unless it is a prescribed preprofessional course), but, having chosen, he is regarded as committed to a full mobilization of his talent and energy.

In the segment devoted to cultural imperatives, the student, after college, will not be able to ignore or derogate these requirements. Only in the cultural electives is he a relatively free agent, but there again he will have made a voluntary choice among three widely different curricular categories. The main incentive for pursuing the electives is that of personal growth. In the electives the instructor can afford "to teach and teach," without bedeviling the student with recitations and tests. A semester achievement examination buttressed by a performance, production, or project (perhaps on a cooperative basis among several students) would suffice for marking purposes.

In summary, the *specialization* is what the student most wants and can scarcely be pulled away from. The *imperatives* are what the university insists upon, following the demands of society. The *electives*, taken in some depth, are sought as a means of cultural satisfaction.

CHAPTER TEN

Graduate Work

It has become a commonplace to observe that, where it once took a high school diploma to get a good job, it now takes a bachelor's degree. It may soon become just as commonplace to say that an advanced degree, a master's or even a doctor's, is essential. In many of our highly technological new industries it already is, even for some relatively low-level positions.

The "getting a good job" angle, however, is far from the only important aspect of advanced academic training. Another is that *good jobs need to be done*, not only in science and technology but in sociology and economics, in philosophy and the arts, as well. So dizzying is the rate at which new knowledge is piling up that advanced training, with the research that this implies, is the only way we can even hope to keep up.

That Land-Grant institutions are among the front-runners in graduate work, producing their share and more of the nation's holders of advanced degrees, cannot be doubted. Although they enroll only about one-fifth of all college students, they account for twice that fraction of the doctorates awarded each year. "It seems clear," said the late Conrad A. Elvehjem at Kansas City, "that the Land-Grant institutions have been extraordinarily successful in graduate work."

Elvehjem, president of the University of Wisconsin until his death in mid-1962, served as over-all evaluator of graduate work. Joining with him as evaluators of graduate work were three men from outside the Land-Grant system noted in the three general areas of endeavor into which work at this level is commonly divided: Bernard Berelson, director of the Bureau of Applied Social Research of Columbia University, in the social sciences; Detlev W. Bronk, president of the Rockefeller Institute and of the National Academy of Sciences, in the natural sciences; Whitney J. Oates, director of the Council of Humanities, Princeton University, in the humanities.

To proceed first with Elvehjem's over-all appraisal: after remarking that the Land-Grant institutions have been "extraordinarily successful in graduate work," Elvehjem continued: "Why they have been so is not so obvious." The climate for leadership, he believed, sprang from "the establishment of the agricultural experiment stations which formalized and recognized research in our institutions for more than three quarters of a century." But, he quickly added:

I believe that the recognition of research—particularly the applied sort of research which was implied in the name *experiment station,* was not as important in the development of quality graduate programs as was the early recognition in these institutions of the fact that basic research must underlie the applications.

Particularly in those institutions in which the college of agriculture was lodged on the same campus with the main state university was there an awareness that problems of production could be solved only through basic studies in such fields as chemistry, physics, biology and so forth. . . . In this connection, I can speak from experience. I received my Ph.D. in a college of agriculture in 1927 and for 30 years I carried on research and trained more than 80 Ph.D.s, and during this period I was never once asked to deviate from basic research in order to solve immediate practical problems. Yet out of these studies came a host of applications—more, I am sure, than if we had held to strictly problem-solving work.

The institution at which Elvehjem obtained his doctorate and at which he did his research was, of course, the University of Wisconsin. And his basic work in the field of biochemistry resulted in practical applications of, among other things, the vitamin B complex.

"Graduate teaching," Elvehjem said, "is research . . . a student working with a professor, a professor working with a student, to learn together, to organize a body of knowledge, to create, and to report."

Accepting this definition, and granting that Land-Grant universities as a group have been extraordinarily successful in meeting it, realistically it can hardly be expected that all Land-Grant institutions will be extraordinarily successful in all phases of graduate work. The fact is that they are not, and that for many of them it would be folly to attempt to offer full across-the-board graduate education.

There are several reasons for this. One is that in some states enrollment is so small that it would be impracticable. The University of Delaware, for instance, with a total residential enrollment of only a little over 3,000, has undertaken doctoral work in only a very few fields—the ones it feels it can do well—and it does them excellently.

Another point which must be considered is that some states support more than one university. While the University of Missouri, for instance, is "the Land-Grant *and* state university," and as such offers a well-rounded program of graduate work, a different situation is found in, say, Indiana.

In Indiana, Purdue is the Land-Grant institution. Indiana University is non-Land-Grant. As a matter of avoiding duplication, Purdue is charged with graduate work in theoretical and applied science for the most part, and Indiana with graduate work in the humanities. Neither can be said to be "well-rounded" in the usual terms, but each is a great university, and *between them* the people of the state of Indiana are well served.

Much that can be said about range of graduate offerings in Land-Grant and other public universities can, as a matter of fact, also be said about some of our most distinguished private institutions. To make a random comparison: Princeton does not offer the science work that is to be found at the California Institute of Technology, nor does Caltech offer the humanities for which Princeton is noted.

Also important in examining graduate work at Land-Grant institutions, particularly in states with limited resources, is the fact that up until fairly recent years a number attempted no graduate work at all. Some have been offering doctorates only since the late 1950's. These institutions—the University of Georgia is an example—have been extremely conservative about going into graduate work until they are properly staffed. Many of the separate Negro Land-Grant institutions in the southern and border states remain at the undergraduate level, and probably will for some time. However, almost without exception, the graduate schools of the other Land-Grant universities in these states are now open to Negroes.

It is within the context of all these circumstances that any analysis of graduate work at Land-Grant institutions must be considered.

Berelson, in his evaluation of graduate work in the social sciences, acknowledged this. Although at one point he summarized that "the Land-Grant institutions include some of the *better* social science departments, but not many of the *very best.* . . . Some do not even pretend to carry on graduate work of any significance," he also noted that many did not enter the graduate field until rather late and that in any case numbers do not tell the whole story. In view of this, he said, "they have done their share and are keeping up their share."

Berelson began his paper by citing the findings of certain statistical and other studies. First was the survey by the U.S. Office of Education of Ph.D.'s produced in the academic year 1958-59. In that year five Land-Grant universities were among the nation's top producers of doctorates and master's degrees in the social sciences, including psychology. California (Berkeley and Los Angeles campuses) awarded 84 Ph.D.'s, Minnesota 80, Wisconsin 58, Ohio State 50, Illinois 44. At the master's level, the same five universities awarded 223, 128, 109, 90, and 87 degrees, respectively. All told, Land-Grant institutions accounted for a third of all social science doctorates that year, about a fourth of the M.A.'s.

Berelson then cited several studies indicative of the quality of work by Land-Grant graduate schools in his field. In the "Keniston Survey" of 1957, for example, six of the 15 universities top-rated in the social sciences were Land-Grant: the Berkeley campus of California fourth, Minnesota seventh, Cornell ninth, Wisconsin tenth, Los Angeles campus of California twelfth, Illinois thirteenth. (In this survey, Professor Hayward Keniston of the University of Pennsylvania asked department heads throughout the country to rate universities in several areas, including social sciences.)

In a survey of his own, the results of which he disclosed for the first time at the Kansas City meeting, Berelson uncovered some interesting facts about the academic training of some leading social scientists. He asked several experts in sociology, anthropology, psychology, and other fields what they thought were the outstanding research reports in each of these fields over 25 years. More than 600 papers were nominated, and Berelson analyzed them in different ways. One way was to list the universities where the authors did the work that earned them the nominations. The familiar names appeared again. California (Berkeley), Minnesota, Illinois, Massachusetts Institute of Technology, Cornell, and Wisconsin were among the 15 most often mentioned—but they were all behind Harvard, Chicago, Columbia, and Yale. Of the 15 institutions where most of the authors received their graduate training, five were Land-Grant. "Good," Berelson commented, "but not great."

Another significant finding emerged from work Berelson had done on his book, *Graduate Education in the United States,* published a year before the Kansas City meeting. At

Kansas City he presented publicly for the first time some comparisons among Land-Grant universities, other public universities, and private universities, as reflected in replies to questionnaires he had sent out.

He found that among Land-Grant recipients of the Ph.D. in social sciences a Land-Grant university had been first choice in fewer cases than had private universities among people who took their degrees in such institutions. A Land-Grant university had been more often selected because of low cost and employment opportunities than because of prestige of the university. Moreover, Land-Grant people were much less inclined than private university people to list their own departments among the first or second best in the nation. More often they would rank them from third to fifth.

There were wide differences, too, in the attitudes of faculty members. Members of Land-Grant graduate faculties almost universally held that their universities not only could but should expand graduate level work. Returns to Berelson's questionnaire indicated that Land-Grant faculties spent 22 per cent of their time "only" or "mainly" on graduate instruction—just a little over half the time spent at this level of instruction by private university faculty members.

Nevertheless, Land-Grant institutions came out very well in responses to this question to recipients of the Ph.D. from various types of institutions: "Taking everything into account, how do you feel about the graduate work leading to your doctorate—what you got out of it compared with what it cost in time, energy, and money?"

About 36 per cent of Land-Grant Ph.D.'s in social sciences said they were "very satisfied," as against 28 per cent of those from other public and 29 per cent of those from private institutions. Half of the Land-Grant group considered that their doctoral programs had been "very good" in training them for their *present jobs*, against 43 and 45 per cent of the others.

Strictly in terms of numbers, Berelson was disturbed that "the social science side of the Land-Grant campus lags behind the natural science side." In 1958-59, the Land-Grant institutions awarded 54 per cent of all doctorates in the biological sciences ("the tie to agriculture," Berelson observed, "is important here"), and 44 per cent in the physical sciences, including mathematics and engineering, as against only about 33 per cent in the social sciences as a whole.[1] Even so, he pointed out, the humanities have fared even worse than the social sciences, a matter which was of sore concern to Oates in his examination of Land-Grant work in the humanities.

Berelson also noted that "the Land-Grant universities are rather heavy on the applied side" of social sciences, awarding nearly two-thirds of all doctorates in that area. "Much of that proportion," he pointed out, however, "is accounted for by agricultural economics, which seems to me an altogether appropriate subject for emphasis in such institutions." Moreover, he said,

My advice is that you not be unduly concerned about this emphasis, certainly that you not be embarrassed over it. . . .

In the first place, there is the *raison d'être* of the Land-Grant institutions themselves, with their interest in what the university can do for the practical affairs of man. I know you take that seriously, and I do too; indeed, I think the entire country should glory in the fact.

Beyond that, however, there are . . . clear signs, in one after another of the social science disciplines, of the development of what, to use a more acceptable term than applied or practical, I can best call professional interests, set alongside academic ones.

As examples of this sort of thing, Berelson cited public administration, clinical psychology, and applied social research among others. "It is not too much to say, I think," he continued, "that we are witnessing, in a rough way, a parallel to the development of engineering in relation to

[1] In 1959-60 these percentages were 55.2, 47.5, and 28.5 respectively.

the physical sciences, or of medicine and agriculture in relation to biology."

Noting that, particularly in engineering and agriculture, these developments have been in large part contributions of the Land-Grant system, Berelson concluded: "This field may represent for the Land-Grant institutions, the same challenge that the sciences represented 100 years ago—the challenge of a growing set of subjects of great importance for human welfare and appropriate for development at a range of graduate schools that have not yet approached their maximum size."

In the natural sciences, as Berelson stated, Land-Grant universities are far stronger than in the social sciences. In the 1958-59 academic year they awarded 44 per cent of all doctorates in physical sciences—45 per cent of those in chemistry, 63 in earth sciences (not including geology, geophysics, or oceanography), 49 in engineering, 40 in geology, 38 in mathematics and statistics, 53 in metallurgy, and 38 in physics. They awarded 38 per cent of the master's degrees.[2]

In the biological sciences, the Land-Grant universities do even better. In 1958-59 they produced 54 per cent of the Ph.D.'s in this field—including 97 per cent of those in pathology and plant pathology, 94 per cent of those in entomology, and 91 per cent of those in genetics. They awarded 47 per cent of the M.A. degrees in biological sciences, with the highest percentages in the same three fields as at the Ph.D. level.[3]

Again, as with social sciences, familiar names appear. The Massachusetts Institute of Technology alone awarded 189 doctorates in physical sciences in 1958-59. California awarded 156, Illinois 133, Wisconsin 73, and Purdue 72. Among them these five Land-Grant universities accounted

[2] In 1959-60 Land-Grant universities conferred 47.5 per cent of all Ph.D.'s in the physical sciences, including engineering and mathematics, and 33.7 of all M.A.'s.

[3] In 1959-60 the percentages were 55.2 for Ph.D.'s and 44.5 for M.A.'s.

that year for a solid 22 per cent of all degrees awarded in physical sciences in the nation.

In biological sciences, California with 105 doctorates, Wisconsin with 81, Illinois with 41, Cornell with 40, and Minnesota with 34 contributed just short of 30 per cent of such degrees.

As for quality of work in the natural sciences at Land-Grant institutions, it need only be noted that of 42 American winners of the Nobel Prize living in 1961, 25 obtained one or more degrees at Land-Grant institutions—and not all of them at those mentioned in the preceding two paragraphs. Of these Nobel laureates, 23 were scientists—of whom eight were currently at work on Land-Grant campuses.

A classic example of the "open door to education" policy of the Land-Grant universities, in fact, and of their eminence in pure scientific research, is Dr. Selman A. Waksman. As a youthful Russian immigrant, Waksman earned his bachelor's and master's degrees at Rutgers and his Ph.D. at California. He won the Nobel Prize in 1952 for his discovery of streptomycin while working at the New Jersey Agricultural Experiment Station.

Streptomycin is only one of a long list of contributions to mankind's welfare which have emerged from the Land-Grant system. Among others are dicumarol (the anti-blood-clotting substance which has saved many a human life and which under another name, warfarin, is one of our most potent rat-killers), the cyclotron, the transistor, the television tube, and several chemical elements. Basic work on fatigue of metals, which has saved the nation's railroads millions of dollars, was done at a Land-Grant university, as well as work that has contributed to the growth of hundreds of other industries, from ceramics to soybean processing.

So it was not an exaggeration for Detlev Bronk to point out at Kansas City: "The original objectives of Land-Grant colleges and universities, extended to the graduate education of large numbers of young men and women, are as essential to the vitality of our national life today as was undergraduate education in 1862. . . . It will be recorded in the history of higher education that one of America's great contributions has been the creation of graduate schools of excellence for many within your universities."

Significantly, Bronk made a strong plea for "an atmosphere wherein the relations of science to art and literature and history and the social sciences can be stressed."

"We need more scientists who are humanists," he said. "Thorough comprehension of a limited sphere of literature and mastery of certain experimental techniques or intellectual tools is an essential part of the educational process; it is the primary objective of many who are to be scientific technicians. For those who are to be scientific scholars and scientific leaders, it is not enough."

How some Land-Grant universities are already responding to this sort of challenge in their requirements for liberal arts and humanities work by students in such scientifically oriented areas as engineering and agriculture will be brought out in the later chapters of this volume which deal with those areas.

Whitney Oates, in his critique of Land-Grant graduate work in the humanities, approached the same point in a somewhat different way. Rather than placing the whole burden for lack of intellectual intercourse between scientists and humanists on the scientists, he declared:

Humanists in the past, I believe, have erred in that they have attempted to define their enterprise in exclusive terms. Rather, it seems to me, the humanities must be regarded inclusively, in the sense that there is no activity of the mind that is without its important humanistic aspects. In other words, the humanities amount to more than the study of the arts, letters, history, philosophy and religion. More importantly they reflect an attitude of mind, call it broadly "philosophical," which pervades, or should, the activities of a university.

Oates quoted an aeronautical engineer friend of his who had remarked that his work proceeded most satisfactorily in a certain institution with a strong humanistic tradition, because, "after all, the ideal of pure research is not in itself scientific but humanistic." If this be the case, Oates continued, "it seems absolutely essential that the humanities must flourish, and in the graduate school, in Land-Grant institutions whose major purpose may well be the pursuit of the agricultural and mechanic arts."

"Clearly," he said at another point, "it is relevant here to take note of the efforts of the Massachusetts Institute of Technology to develop its curriculum in the humanities and social studies."

How do Land-Grant universities measure up to Oates's criteria? Oates cited first some data from the *Index to Doctoral Dissertations* for 1959-60. In that year 1,092 Ph.D.'s were awarded in history, literature, and philosophy, 209 of them—or slightly less than 20 per cent—by Land-Grant graduate schools. Among other universities, Harvard, Yale, Princeton, Columbia, and Chicago alone awarded 314, or nearly 30 per cent. Analyzing the distribution of Land-Grant degrees, Oates found that 140 of them, or about 70 per cent, were awarded by California, Illinois, Minnesota, and Wisconsin.

Oates expressed little patience with those who would dismiss these institutions' pre-eminence in the humanities simply on the basis that they are big and can afford the luxury of offering work in this field. Commitment, he felt, is important too. "To be sure," he said, "these excellent Land-Grant universities are indeed large, *but* it should not be forgotten that they have determined to have a balanced intellectual bill of fare. After all, it is within their power to spend the money now allocated to the humanities on other areas. The fact remains that they have decided not to."

In quality, Oates assured his listeners, humanities graduate work by the best of the Land-Grant institutions is on a par with that of the "prestige" private institutions. Indicative of this was Oates's analysis of the choices which Woodrow Wilson Fellowship winners made of the institutions where they would take graduate work leading to teaching careers, the purpose of these fellowships. From 1945 to 1961, he found, 801 Wilson fellows, a little over 20 per cent of them, chose to work at 30 different Land-Grant institutions. As might be expected, large numbers went to California (266), Illinois (53), Minnesota (65), and Wisconsin (143), but substantial contingents also went to Cornell (128), MIT (62) and Ohio State (19). "It would seem to be no accident," Oates said, "that these Wilson fellows selected these seven admittedly excellent Land-Grant universities in such large numbers."

How to strengthen Land-Grant graduate work in the humanities? Oates recommended as the first step to "strengthen the programs for master's degrees in the humanistic fields in those institutions which as yet have not fully developed doctoral programs."

Between the academic years 1956-57 and 1958-59, he reported, 13 Land-Grant institutions increased their awards of M.A.'s by 25 to 50 per cent. These, predictably, included California, Illinois, Ohio State, and Wisconsin, but "the other nine," Oates observed, "institutions like the University of Connecticut, the University of Georgia, Louisiana State, Michigan State, Rutgers and West Virginia University, show such marked increases in the number of master's degrees granted that it must reflect a conscious effort to improve humanistic graduation."

Emphasizing that he recommended development of master's programs only as a first step, Oates stressed the need for doctoral programs as well. For one thing, he stated his "firm conviction that a teacher-scholar, no matter what his field, needs that amount of advanced education which culminates in the compounding of a doctoral dissertation before he is ready to embark on his professional career as a teacher-scholar. Anything short of this would amount to saying that a medical student is ready to be a practicing doctor as soon as he has finished his course in anatomy."

What, then, is the posture of the Land-Grant universities in the all-important field of graduate work as they enter their second century? President Henry of Illinois, in his summarizing speech at Kansas City, put it this way:

The general need is clearly set forth by President Elvehjem. The National Science Foundation estimates, for example, that if the current trend is to be maintained, we will need twice as many scientists in 1970 as now. Including replacements and additions, we shall need 346,000 new college teachers in the next 10 years, compared with the present full-time roster of 286,000. Of the 16 colleges that produce a quarter of the nation's college teachers in liberal arts and education, 11 are state universities. Thus, in addition to anticipating the supply of scientists, our institutions must also train a large portion of the college teachers and continue to do their share for the elementary and secondary schools. All of this is without reference to increased numbers of foreign students and increased travel abroad for faculty.

Henry then quoted a key paragraph from Elvehjem's speech:

Can we manage? Can our faculties with all their outside distractions, their advisory groups in government, their foundation panels, their consultantships, their fragmented scientific meetings, and all the rest, spread themselves and multiply their ranks in quality as well as number to meet the need? Can they maintain and improve the quality of undergraduate work simultaneously—so that as the great undergraduate tide reaches the doors of graduate schools, it is prepared for higher level work? It will be a real test.

To which Henry replied: "We must try."

CHAPTER ELEVEN

Agriculture, Home Economics, and Veterinary Medicine

Although the appellation "cow college" has long since lost whatever derisive validity it may once have had, agriculture remains a prime concern for the Land-Grant institutions, and not only because the Morrill Act stipulated that they must teach it. On every Land-Grant campus is found a genuine dedication to the welfare of the farmer and the land.

Most of the nation's schools or colleges of agriculture—all but a scant half-dozen—are operated by the 68 Land-Grant institutions. In educational areas traditionally associated with agriculture, half of the bachelor's and advanced degrees in home economics are awarded by 60 Land-Grant institutions, and 16 of the nation's 18 schools of veterinary medicine are operated by these institutions. They award over 90 per cent of the D.V.M. degrees.

In their time the "ag" schools have contributed importantly to the developments which have made American agriculture the most prosperous and efficient on earth. As just one evidence of this, today the direct labor of less than 10 per cent of the population is needed to feed the nation. A century ago, when the Morrill Act was passed, half of the nation worked on farms to feed the other half and itself.

Without question, the three-pronged Land-Grant approach to learning through *instruction, research,* and *extension* has reached its highest peak of perfection in the schools and colleges of agriculture. "They have educated a multitude of capable individuals who could not have obtained advanced learning from other schools," said Earl Coke, the "outside" evaluator of agriculture, at Kansas City. "Through their research they have provided the basis for agriculture's 'technical revolution,' which in turn freed millions of people from the land to take part in the phenomenal economic growth of our past century. These institutions have led the way in bringing the colleges to the people through adult education and 4-H Club work. Their 'campuses' have truly become statewide."

But, continued Coke, "it has been difficult for the colleges, as it has for all institutions, to keep pace with the revolutionary changes of recent years. The recognized lag has caused some impatience both inside and outside the agricultural colleges. Yet, we find, too, a frequent reluctance to change."

As outside evaluator, Coke was only one of three men who presented special studies on agricultural education at the Centennial Convocation. The other two were Paul A. Miller, then provost of Michigan State University and now president of West Virginia University, and Theodore W. Schultz, professor of agricultural economics at the University of Chicago. Miller acted as "inside" evaluator of agricultural education, and Schultz, who brought to his task 13 years of previous experience at the Land-Grant Iowa State University, presented an analysis of the other two papers.

Among the three men there was no disagreement with such of Coke's views as have been quoted thus far, that the Land-Grant agricultural schools have contributed importantly and with distinction to the nation's development. From there on, however, they parted company in some important details.

To proceed first with Coke's views: wherein does he feel that change is called for, and what changes does he propose? Noting, with respect to resident instruction, that "most of today's agricultural students will work in businesses allied to agricultural production," and that "those who do go into farming must deal with problems that were of little or no importance 20 or even 10 years ago," he stated flatly: "The needed changes in training required by agricultural students have not taken place. . . . The agricultural college curricula are still largely devoted to offerings in technical agriculture. Courses of study are limited to a narrow segment by major requirements." (One agricultural school, Coke found, listed 25 majors, against four in the same university's engineering school.)

Technical agriculture, Coke said, "should continue to be the basic offering of the agricultural colleges, but with the students having considerable latitude in selecting courses in their field of interest. Undergraduate instruction should make the students aware of major goals, problems and fundamental findings of a discipline rather than to train each one as a specialist or practitioner."

Moreover, Coke continued, even with technical subjects the basis for agricultural education, "all undergraduate students, regardless of their major interests or ultimate occupation, should have training in the social sciences, life sciences, physical sciences and the humanities. . . . Curricula must be broad enough to provide the basic tools of analysis, expression and understanding."

In connection with the last point, Coke called especially for "training in communication, both written and spoken," for agriculture students no less than for any kind of student. "The ability to communicate effectively," he said, "can make a tremendous difference in personal happiness and business success."

That farming is indeed a business these days—a way of making a living rather than simply a way of life as it was in days gone by—led Coke to one of his most important final recommendations: "That most students be encouraged to take courses providing a basic understanding of finance, management and organization."

"It makes little difference," Coke continued, "whether the student plans to farm, to enter some agricultural business, or become an educator. This type of training is of major importance. . . .

"The agricultural colleges have done little to provide business training for their students. It is imperative that this be done. If it cannot be done within the agricultural college, students must have easy access to the schools of business administration."

Miller, while not differing significantly with Coke on this matter, viewed it from a somewhat different perspective—concerning himself more with the philosophical orientation of agricultural education rather than with "how-to-do-it" recommendations for changes in curriculum.

Noting early in his paper that "the agricultural colleges emerged from the requirements of national purpose and have remained close to it," he developed over the next few paragraphs a theme summarized in these words:

The agricultural colleges are now involved in a society and world community which have problems so interrelated that they form into larger and larger combines while simultaneously the knowledge and skills by which to solve them break down into smaller and smaller fragments. . . .

The agricultural colleges do not and cannot command such a large amount of the total store of expertise on agricultural affairs as they once did. Beginning with the new [governmental] agencies of the thirties, there followed the proliferation of permanently entrenched agencies of specialized technical competence. This is especially true in the private sector: Applied research programs and the employment of specialists by feed and fertilizer companies, commercial spray firms, private consulting firms. . . .

Moreover, Miller said, the agricultural schools have kept pace neither with what is happening to the intellectual "disciplines" or with the "recasting of national goals" that has come with the shift of political weight to the cities.

With respect to the intellectual disciplines, Miller observed that "the recent breakthroughs in science and technology result increasingly from such mergers as, for example, between biology, chemistry and physics," but that the Land-Grant agricultural schools exhibit "a growing inability to form new combinations."

With reference to national goals, Miller found that urban shifts, "especially in periods of unemployment and small business failure, have made it appear that agriculture, and the establishment built around it, seemed to be interested only in itself" and have "placed the agricultural colleges in a climate of problems rather than opportunities."

Schultz concurred with Coke and Miller that the colleges have advanced useful agricultural knowledge through research—"they have far exceeded the most optimistic expectations"—but he was considerably more brusque in his appraisal of their resident instruction.

"Your sector of higher education," he told the assembled deans, "unfortunately produces an educational product that is not good enough in quality. . . . The first 100 years have not given us a single agricultural college that is on a par in quality in its undergraduate instruction with Swarthmore and Oberlin or with California Institute of Technology and Massachusetts Institute of Technology."

A prime reason for this, Schultz declared, is that "the doors of colleges and universities have been opened wide to the faculty to earn outside income. This dilution of full-time residence and the erosion in competence in the faculty because non-academic bidders acquire much of the best talent, is reducing the quality of instruction."

As for revision of curricula, Schultz agreed with Coke by saying that they "are too narrowly devoted to technical agriculture," but he quarreled with what he called Coke's "plea for more of the same—a new mixture of technical courses to train students for agricultural processing, marketing and . . . the Madison Avenue art of communication."

The answer to curricula problems, Schultz felt, falls rather in the area of the intellectual perspective discussed by Miller. "The cultural and intellectual attributes of science and technology have become a strong force affecting higher education," he said. "The influence of this force runs much in your favor because of your comparative advantage in science and technology. But the agricultural colleges have not capitalized on the cultural and intellectual attributes of science and technology."

This, he said, is because of the "notion that our society is split into two cultures, one based on science and the other on the humanities." Both are essential, he said; "the real choice pertains to how they are to be taught."

It is true that the findings of Coke, Miller, and Schultz could be widely applied to resident instruction in agriculture today. It is also true, however, that at least some Land-Grant institutions have been making strenuous efforts to offset the shortcomings these men cited.

Speaking for just one such institution, Professor Karl Gardner, associate dean of the University of Illinois College of Agriculture, observed in an interview: "The criticism that we have provided too much technical and how-to-do training is being overcome. We started some time ago, as did other schools. The decrease in the hours of agricultural work—20 per cent here—leaves more time for the sciences and the humanities, and we have used it for that. Just recently [spring 1962] the university senate accepted a report recommending minimum hours of biology, physics, social sciences, and humanities, plus a foreign language reading requirement, as general requirements for all students."

Mention of this program, with a June 1, 1964, deadline, prompted Dean Louis B. Howard of the Illinois college to comment that "this is a reflection of the attitude of moving toward a definition of agriculture much bigger than farming." But "we don't want to belittle farming in any sense," Howard hastened to add. "We need many more trained men to provide leadership in farm communities."

In recognition of this need for farm leadership, Illinois conducts what Gardner described as "a frank, bare, bald recruitment program."

"We go out and talk it up in a large number of high schools," he explained. "We also have programs here on this campus. High school students come here and hear the same song sung again." This is done also, Gardner emphasized, by numerous other agricultural colleges. Moreover, he added, many other colleges are emphasizing agricultural science along with Illinois, where he said some 20 per cent of all students are enrolled in science-oriented courses, including food processing and the like.

Interestingly, Gardner pointed out, "we had a lot of science, literature and so forth in our curriculum at the turn of the century. There just weren't enough agriculture courses then to fill out. As new agriculture courses were developed we put them in, and some of the other things gave way." "We now realize," Howard added, "that we overshot, but we are getting back to a better balance. A student today takes 50 percent of his work in arts and science."

The Illinois picture is mirrored many places—at Minnesota, for example, where Dean Harold Macy of the university's Institute of Agriculture reminisced: "We used to develop manual skills, plowing, horseshoeing, things like that. Students in animal husbandry used to spend a tremendous amount of time on stock judging."

Today, Dean Macy continued, "vocational courses are still being given, but the content is changing; it isn't *how-to* any more, but *why.* The percentage of our graduates who are going back to the farm is becoming smaller. Our young people are going into banks, the machinery business. All sorts of business firms are coming to us for recruits, and they need people who are educated, not just trained as technicians."

What is happening in agriculture is happening too in instruction in the related areas of home economics and veterinary medicine. Thoughtful leaders in these professions are examining curricula and approaches in the light of present-day and predictable future demands, and some schools, at least, are proceeding to revise their procedures in line with modern concepts. In both areas, greater emphasis is daily being placed on preparing young people to take responsibility as citizens as well as practitioners of a profession.

The evaluator of home economics was Reuben G. Gustavson, who began a long career in education at one Land-Grant institution, Colorado State College (now University), became chancellor of another, the University of Nebraska, and "retired" to teach chemistry at a third, the University of Arizona.

Gustavson examined course offerings in university catalogs of the early 1920's and compared them with present-day offerings. "It is very evident that . . . 40 years ago the home economist paid a good deal of attention to the farm home," he reported at Kansas City, "for example, in the canning of foods." By contrast, "the catalogs of the last decade reveal a new emphasis . . . the very complicated problems of child development . . . the family as a unit . . . the development of good citizens as a partial end-result of sound family relations. . . . All of these problems are reflected in home economics curricula now."

The traditional home economics areas are still definitely present in today's curriculum, however, and Gustavson found among the department heads to whom he sent a questionnaire "those who feel that there should be a decreased emphasis on the skills of 'sewing and cooking.'" Others felt that "since the vast majority of the young women who major in home economics will become homemakers, the undergraduate curriculum should take care of this high probability." All in all, Gustavson concluded, "there is a live discussion taking place on the curriculum in home economics with no uniformity of decision."

Uniformity of decision aside, home economics curricula are nonetheless undergoing change, and in some cases strikingly. As just one instance, the College of Home Economics of Michigan State University in the fall of 1961 put into effect a new plan under which prescribed home economics courses were slashed from 38 hours to 15. To this was added 45 hours of prescribed work in "American Thought and Language," natural science, social science, and humanities, all taken in the University College rather than the College of Home Economics.

Almost concurrently with MSU, the University of Massachusetts and Kansas State University, as two other examples, were taking similar steps. At Massachusetts a home economics major now must take 75 per cent of her work in the liberal arts division. At Kansas State, required home economics courses now total only 33 hours, with 64 hours required in arts and sciences and electives making up the remaining 27.

"Preparation for home economics jobs demands the right balance of liberal education and professional training," said Dean Marion A. Niederpruem of Massachusetts, in summing up current thought in the field for a Boston women's group in 1962. "We receive letters every day with job offers for home economists. It breaks my heart that we don't have enough young women qualified to take them."

Work in veterinary medicine was evaluated at Kansas City by Dr. William A. Hagan, director of the National Animal Disease Laboratory, a federal government installation at Ames, Iowa. In summary, Hagan found: "The opportunities for a first-class education are now present in all of our schools. Of their own volition for the most part, but stimulated and assisted in many cases by the organized profession, all of our schools are progressing steadily in broadening and improving their teaching and research programs."

Education in veterinary medicine is overseen by the Council on Education of the American Veterinary Medical Association. This council makes no effort to prescribe curricula beyond insisting that each college require a minimum of two years of English, physics, biology, chemistry, social science, and humanities.

Hagan recalled that during the late 1940's and 1950's, a period when eight of the present 18 schools were established, he was surprised to find, as a member of the council, that many Land-Grant colleges "resisted the idea of including the humanities and wished to substitute courses in poultry husbandry, animal husbandry, field crops and other practical agricultural courses."

While he expressed "no objection to these courses as such," he did find them objectionable in these cases because "they forced out general educational courses which, in the long run, would be more useful to the veterinarian as a leader in his community and a well-informed citizen." Fortunately, he added, "this situation has, in large measure, been overcome through insistence by the Council."

As for instruction in the basic scientific subjects, such as pathology and microbiology, which the student veterinarian is required to take, Hagan described it as "not inferior to that given to students of medicine," though he acknowledged that they "have to be somewhat more diffuse and less specialized than those of medical schools" since the veterinarian treats a variety of animals and the physician only one. "There is only one science found in the modern medical school curriculum," he slyly observed, "for which no counterpart can be found in that of veterinary schools. That is psychiatry."

It need hardly be pointed out, of course, that the day when the veterinarian was primarily a "horse doctor" has long ago passed. Nor is it correct to regard him as a dog and cat doctor. The modern veterinarian is an important member of the health team. He not only keeps livestock healthy and productive on the farm but inspects animal food products for the safety of the public.

A widening field of veterinary medicine, linked with human medicine, is in what are called the "zoonoses," animal diseases which are transmissible to man. There are more than 100 known zoonoses. Some of the better known ones are rabies, sleeping sickness, undulant fever, and Rocky Mountain spotted fever.

It was veterinary research which discovered that what had been supposed to be three different diseases in cattle, swine, and goats, were caused by the same type of organism—the same type that causes undulant fever in humans. By 1959, further research had controlled the disease in cows to the extent that the incidence in humans was only one-seventh of what it had been 10 years earlier.

In 1917, when American veterinarians began a campaign against tuberculosis in cows, one out of every 20 animals was infected. Today this has been cut to about one out of every 500—and over the five years 1956-60 fewer than 10 persons were reported suffering from tuberculosis attributable to milk supply. In some parts of the world 65 per cent or more of the human tuberculosis cases are traced to cows.

It is just this widening of the demands on the veterinary profession that gave Dr. Hagan his only cause for real concern. Gratified as he was, generally speaking, about the quality of veterinary education, he expressed misgivings about the quantity of it. "I will hazard the guess," he said, "that perhaps three times the present number of veterinarians will be needed to meet the needs of the country by 1980."

At present the 18 veterinary colleges are turning out between 900 and 1,000 practitioners and researchers per year, and Dr. Hagan saw little prospect that this could be increased much, certainly not enough to meet indicated needs by 1980.

Thus far in this chapter, discussion has been largely confined to resident instruction in agriculture and its two historically related areas of home economics and veterinary medicine. Resident instruction, however, is far from the whole story in agricultural education. Through cooperative extension, further education has for 50 years been brought to the farmer and his wife, and, through the 4-H Clubs, to his children.

Cooperative extension is financed jointly through the U.S. Department of Agriculture, the Land-Grant schools and colleges of agriculture, and, in some cases, state departments of agriculture. It is carried out at the grass roots by "county agents," many of whom have rather large staffs, including specialists in home economics and other fields. It has been monumentally successful in disseminating information, and still is. Yet it too has come under scrutiny in recent years as the complexion of rural America has changed. In Earl Coke's words:

> As long as the Nation's basic need was for more food and fiber, there was an unquestioned singleness of purpose with the agricultural college and its supporters. However, to a considerable degree, commercial agriculture has grown past agricultural extension. We find farmers looking to the research worker or the commercial specialist for advice . . . in specific technical information such as fertilizer recommendations and animal feeding practices.
>
> The agricultural colleges should help the "commercial specialists" to keep currently informed on technical developments in his field. As these specialists succeed in shortening the gap between the discovery of new facts through research and their application on the farm, they perform a valuable service to society."

Most important, however, Coke said, "they also make it possible for colleges to give greater emphasis to other important educational programs."

Chief among the "other important educational programs" which Coke believes might well be carried afield by the agricultural colleges is that of farm management. Evolution of agriculture into its modern form, he explained, with growing interdependence of its production and business aspects, "means that many problems of the farmer originate off the farm and many problems of business start on the farm."

"I strongly urge," he said, "that college farm management teams make liberal use of the banker, the merchant and the processor in their educational efforts. In the course of this cooperative effort college people, too, will better understand the total farm management problem."

As with resident instruction, so with extension. What

Coke recommended is under way in the more forward-looking schools. Iowa State University and North Carolina State College are operating "agricultural adjustment centers" which, with substantial foundation support, are working to help the farmers of their states adjust to a new kind of world in terms of prices, new production practices, and the like. Off campus services are involved too.

"Our extension work is changing substantially," said Howard at Illinois, adding:

We now are more and more using our extension specialists to get information to other people who will pass it along—the seed dealer, for instance. Dealers, our own field men and others —500 or 600 people at a time—will come in here for a week or so to learn about sprays, how to spray, what and when. Then they will go home and pass this along. Bankers will come in for similar sessions on agricultural credit.

The role of the county agent has changed. We recognize that no man can any longer be a specialist in all areas. We have begun to back him up with "area advisors." We put a man into a several-county area who knows all about swine, for instance, or dairy cows. We have people who know about farm and home management too, in terms of the total resources of a family unit, who can advise when it would be better economically to remodel the barn and when it would be better to remodel the house.

Chapter 3 of this volume took up the activities by representative Land-Grant institutions in community affairs— deferring until this chapter, however, the related problems associated with rural areas and what Land-Grant people are doing about them. The trends insofar as they affect people on the farm have just been sketched, but there is another facet to the rural area question, one which is just as critical as those involving actual farming, and which falls within the purview of cooperative extension.

Senator George D. Aiken of Vermont, in remarks at the Land-Grant system's one hundredth birthday observance in Washington, July 2, 1962, brought it up in these words: "In only one sphere of our domestic growth does it seem we have failed to avail ourselves of the Land-Grant tools we need to develop our human resources. This is in our small rural communities. Many of these communities are withering on the vine as their young people move to the cities in search of greater opportunities. We should do more to provide these small communities with adequate tools for maintaining productive industry in their home towns."

The communities to which Aiken referred are not the "fringe area" communities, in transition from rural to suburban, which were discussed in Chapter 3. They are those beyond the metropolitan fringe, in areas still unabashedly rural.

J. B. Claar, associate director of extension at the University of Illinois, in a speech at the Country Life meeting, posed the issue this way: "In order to have a vigorous and dynamic [rural] community it is highly desirable, if not essential, to have a balance between commercial farming and industrial development. . . . Areas which depend on agriculture alone tend to be characterized by an aging population and economic activity that lags behind other areas."

As might be expected from Claar's remarks, his own university is one among several Land-Grant institutions which are aware of the problems of communities in some rural areas. Dean Howard, continuing his review of the evolving cooperative extension structure at Illinois, said:

Another change is that we help meet the problems of rural communities where people have migrated out. We work in area resource development. In Southern Illinois, in an eight-county area, we have set up regional and county committees, staffed with a man and a woman, to help people examine and evaluate what is happening and will happen—what is happening to their young people, how to extend their economic base. Some possibilities include the processing of strawberries raised in this area, and the development of recreational areas, bringing in outside money from hunting and fishing or from the Southern Illinois equivalent of a dude ranch.

For many an American farmer and small-town resident, awareness of agricultural extension dawned with the 4-H

Club. This far-flung organization, with its four-leaf clover insignia symbolizing Head, Heart, Hands, and Health, today enrolls some 2,350,000 youngsters as members. In rural areas its status remains clear and its functions clear-cut. As rural blends with fringe, however, and fringe with suburb, both status and function become confused.

Coke approached the matter by asking two questions: Is 4-H designed to serve urban and suburban areas? Should an organization receiving important public money compete with privately supported organizations (such as the Boy Scouts)?

Emphasizing that although 4-H is often called a youth organization, but is in reality "a program through which the Land-Grant institutions provide interested youth with learning opportunities not readily available to them elsewhere," Coke recommended:

1. Continued strong effort to obtain the participation of a larger portion of rural youth in 4-H Club work.

2. Extending 4-H Club programs, as funds and personnel permit, to more suburban and urban areas.

3. Funds from private sources . . . to expand this work, especially to urban and suburban children.

An example of a really urban 4-H activity is to be found in Chicago, where the Illinois Cooperative Extension Service sponsors some 50 groups, with assistance from private donations, including the poorer areas of the city. Girls engage in the same sort of home economics projects as their rural cousins. The boys keep small animals—even a few cattle at the stockyards—and carry on home and yard improvement projects, projects in electronics, etc. The program was worked out at a conference with other youth groups in the mayor's office in order to avoid overlapping with the Boy Scouts, for example. One advantage seen in 4-H in these poorer areas is that there is no outlay for uniforms and the like.

Coke conceded that "it can be argued with some logic that since 4-H membership is rapidly increasing [in urban areas] the responsibility for this activity should not be with the agricultural colleges." Nevertheless, he said, "I recommend that these colleges continue to direct this program because of . . . the danger of seriously disrupting a successful and important service if the work comes under a different administration."

Turning now to the third facet of the work of agricultural colleges, research—the situation today as seen by Coke, and his recommendations, may best be expressed in the following extract from his paper:

> Most of the demand is for research "to put out fires." There is little insistence on basic research even though its importance is generally recognized. People in agriculture want answers to current problems. Funds have not been sufficient to finance this applied research and also a large program of basic research. If we are to develop the large body of fundamental knowledge needed to make possible the pursuit of applied research, the agricultural colleges must take the initiative. They must convince their supporters of the vital importance of basic research to future progress.

Miller, while recognizing that the colleges' research programs "grew from an immediate response to problems," was not quite so positive as Coke that basic research had been ignored. "The orientation," he said, "has increasingly shifted to an interest in fundamental science."

However, Miller saw another hazard, the same one which he identified as endangering residential instruction—"a growing inability to form new combinations of the disciplines to adjust to the rapid changes in the problems."

"The agricultural colleges," he explained, "combine into a single organization the disciplines—in a response to the ideals of the university—and the commodities—in a response to the nature of human interests in the real world. Though on balance the tension produced by this combination . . . has been healthy, some of the newer frontiers of science, and certain interdisciplinary problems of the world as well, have not easily found a home within it."

Again, as in the case of resident instruction and extension, trails are being blazed in research by certain Land-Grant universities. To take one particularly good illustration, the University of Minnesota's Institute of Agriculture is clearly emphasizing the interdisciplinary approach to research. "My own professorship, for example," Dean Macy pointed out, "is in the school of medicine."

All in all, the Minnesota approach to research furnishes a classic example of the Land-Grant tradition in its blend of the theoretical with the applied. Macy, while expressing himself strongly that "we must do more in basic science," immediately added, "but we must not isolate ourselves from its application. There is nothing undignified about applied research. It is the wedding of the two where Land-Grant institutions can make a contribution.

"I think there is a rich possibility in and among Land-Grant institutions to get brains and a variety of talents both within an institution and from others. If we put our wits together we can get lots of things done."

In times past, much of the research by agricultural colleges was what Macy called "just testing things—half a dozen kinds of milk strainers, or different kinds of chemical compounds."

"We are trying to keep away from projects like that," he explained. "We still must do some evaluation of the animals and plants we develop here, of course, but otherwise we emphasize the *why* in our research. For example, we have a man doing research on the cuticle of insects [a tough membrane lining the outer shell], often using the electron microscope. Out of this may come new knowledge on why and how certain insecticides act as they do."

At the Illinois Agricultural Experiment Station, Professor Tom S. Hamilton, associate director, recalled:

Like most colleges, up to 1945 we were principally concerned with telling the farmer how to raise more food. We changed dramatically and suddenly to a type of research much more basic—not to increase the quantity of food, but the quality, and to increase the efficiency of agriculture. Things like—

A super sweet corn which soon will replace most of the other varieties. . . .

Field corn highly resistant to northern leaf blight. We noted a dominant gene in one kind of corn which could be very quickly put into almost all other standard kinds. . . .

A scab-resistant apple. We took a gene from a crab apple which resists scab and transferred it to other apples. Soon we will no longer have to spray for scab. . . .

Leaner meat animals. We used to have to slaughter an animal to find out how much fat it had. Now we know that potassium has an affinity for fatty tissues. We feed an animal radioactive potassium, and it shows up in detecting machines. The value of this is in working out feeding programs and selecting breeding stock.

CHAPTER TWELVE

Engineering

The second of the three broad areas which the Morrill Act stipulated be taught in the new Land-Grant colleges was what was called, in the quaint language of the time, the "mechanic arts."

In those days the mechanic arts included much of the work of the machinist and construction worker. About as complicated a piece of mechanical equipment as had been designed and built up to then was the steam locomotive. Already, however, it was apparent to Justin Morrill and some of his contemporaries that scientific knowledge was beginning to increase at a geometric rate and that the time was coming when the nation would need hundreds of thousands of men who knew how to use it.

What Morrill called the mechanic arts we today call engineering, and today one-third, or 52 out of 157, of all American engineering schools with accredited curricula are at Land-Grant institutions. As for their production of engineers, Dean Frederick C. Lindvall of the California Institute of Technology, who served as outside evaluator of engineering instruction, pointed out at Kansas City that this third grants nearly half of the bachelor's degrees in this field. Moreover, he noted, the 28 Land-Grant engineering schools which offer the Ph.D. in engineering confer half of those degrees as well.

Even excluding the massive Ph.D. production of the Massachusetts Institute of Technology, an atypical Land-

Grant institution in that it concentrates on the scientific-engineering field, Land-Grant institutions still award a third of engineering Ph.D.'s.

The term "engineering," however, if taken to mean simply the building of bridges and the harnessing of electricity, as it is to a great extent still taken, is hardly an adequate designation in this day and age. Rather than an art, engineering has become a profession. Such a widely respected authority as William L. Everitt, dean of engineering at the Land-Grant University of Illinois, predicts, in fact, that in another 50 years it "will be acknowledged as the most learned profession."

Dean Everitt's view, like that of many another perceptive member of the profession, stems from the conviction that the modern engineer, no less than any other citizen, should be able to function as an intelligent community leader rather than simply as a narrowly trained technologist. It is this widespread conviction that has led to two important trends in recent years in engineering education: (1) increased emphasis on basic science and mathematics; (2) an insistence on more work in liberal arts, social sciences, and the humanities.

With respect to the first point, a rueful sort of joke has been going the rounds in engineering circles for some time now. It is that "engineering diplomas should be printed in some sort of disappearing ink that will be unreadable after about ten years." The root of this witticism is the undeniable fact that so many engineering curricula are loaded with techniques of the moment that often what a student learns is out-of-date by the time he graduates. Hence the effort to reshape engineering into "engineering science" by exposing the student to the basic science and mathematics that will enable him to adapt to any new techniques that develop during his professional career.

With respect to the liberal education of engineers, a significant number of engineering educators feel as did members of a special subcommittee which reported to the

Engineering Division of the Land-Grant association at Kansas City. This committee, headed by Dean J. R. Whinnery of the Berkeley campus of the University of California, called for an approach to engineering that "prepares and motivates the student . . . for the solution of the real and difficult problems of our civilization."

It would be erroneous, however, to assume that either the trend toward the engineering science concept or the trend toward liberalization of the engineering curriculum has taken on anything like prairie-fire proportions. The Engineers Joint Council, in a May 1962 report, stated:

> The engineering curriculum has been the subject of extensive experimentation, but much more remains to be done. Particularly vital is the question of "design" [put in quotation marks in the report because, as an evolving concept, it still means different things to different people, except that all agree it involves both basic and applied science], the extent to which it can be taught, and how it can be taught in academic situations. . . . One of the major requirements is for increased emphasis on education to produce literacy in the social-economic-political field as well as literacy in scientific and technical fields. . . .

Engineering educators reflect the view of the EJC. Professor Eugene S. Ferguson of the mechanical engineering department at Iowa State University, a long-time analyst of engineering education, refers to "the preoccupation with 'efficient' teaching and 'businesslike' schedules which have been characteristic of engineering schools for at least 80 years," to the detriment of a broadly scientific and liberal outlook. Dean A. T. Granger of the University of Tennessee engineering school, in a paper delivered at Kansas City, presented tables indicating that few Land-Grant engineering schools include as much as 10 per cent of English and literature or other nontechnical electives in their curricula. This is markedly short of the 17 per cent average for all engineering schools reported by Earl J. McGrath and Edwin J. Holstein in *Liberal Education and Engineering* in 1960.

Nevertheless, determined starts have been made at a number of universities, including some Land-Grant institutions, and a look at what is being done should be rewarding.

To provide examples of advanced thinking in engineering education, three Land-Grant establishments, the Oakland campus of Michigan State University, the University of Illinois, and the University of Minnesota, were visited.

Selection of these three by no means implies that imaginative approaches to engineering are not being made by some other Land-Grant and non-Land-Grant schools. The plan being evolved by Dean L. M. K. Boelter of the University of California at Los Angeles is one such approach. Boelter's plan, centering on what he calls "resource engineering," is particularly fitting as an area of concentration for a Land-Grant institution, contemplating as it does the management of such items of the people's property as water, minerals, and air, and their interplay with one another as well as with manpower itself. It is cut, really, from the same cloth as Daniel Aldrich's ideas for the new Irvine campus of California, which were reported in Chapter 1 of this volume.

Other examples of tradition-shattering engineering curricula could be cited, but in the overall they are so relatively few that a close look at the three Land-Grant engineering schools listed seems worthwhile. Of these, the one that is probably being most closely watched by engineers is that at MSU Oakland.

Those who recall how Oakland was established in 1959 will recognize the reason for this as the trail-blazing approach with which the entire campus was conceived. In the case of engineering, MSUO concluded that it was time to do something about the "disappearing ink" joke—that the traditional curriculum, with early specialized training in electrical engineering, for instance, or mechanical engineering, should be abandoned in favor of an engineering science approach, with an ample dose of liberal arts.

Although the program is still subject to further experimentation and modification, it will unquestionably continue on the general principle expressed by Chancellor D. B. Varner, who said in an interview during the preparation of this book: "There should be a division of labor between the university and industry in the education of engineers. The part that we can do better is to educate, not train—and to educate a person with a command of engineering fundamentals who we hope can become a literate leader in his profession. A University wastes its resources when it takes on the task of training."

At the time, MSUO had yet to send out its first graduate, in engineering or any other field, but it had been placing students in vacation-time jobs. As support for his belief that "so far, I think we are on target," Varner cited the fact that "one large electronics manufacturer told me the other day 'we will give them on-the-job training, and send them on to MIT or somewhere else for graduate work if they need it, but you give us men like these and we'll be happy.'"

In the science and engineering parts of its program, MSUO is committed to the fundamentals. "We are trying to teach them the basic science that they won't have a chance to learn later," explained William Hammerle, MSUO's scholarly young dean of engineering. "The science courses are integrated into the engineering program. We don't teach chemical engineering, or mechanical engineering, but chemical phenomena and mechanical phenomena. The same with mathematics—our calculus course is designed to get them into physics."

To accommodate its expanded requirements in basic science and liberal arts, MSUO has dispensed with what Hammerle calls "hardware courses"—the laboratories, sometimes virtually shops, where students tear down and reassemble machines and use ponderous apparatus to test the strengths of metals. "The equipment we use," Hammerle said, "is designed to illustrate the *principles* of industrial type equipment. If you give up the idea of studying the industrial type equipment itself you can put a thing on a bench instead of perhaps a 40-foot tower. You can use a piece of copper pipe, for example, instead of a room-size radiator."

Much of the equipment that Hammerle needs cannot be found on the market and has to be built in the engineering building's well-equipped machine shop. This, instead of being a handicap, Hammerle regards as an opportunity to introduce the work in design called for in the EJC report.

"After all," he observed, "we are an engineering school, and design is a fundamental part of engineering. We expect to put some actual design work into the senior year course in analysis and design, which might otherwise be completely a course in applied science. Our first project will be to design apparatus for underclassmen."

Hammerle's disenchantment with "hardware courses" as part of the actual engineering curriculum is shared by his colleagues at Illinois and Minnesota. "We have reduced our drawing, shop and demonstration laboratory courses," Everitt said. "In demonstration labs students used to run a torque speed curve on a compound motor, then on a shunt-wound motor and every other type of motor. When they were through they had a set of curves that were already in a book.

"We emphasize laboratory methods now, but we don't make students prove every curve in the book by experiment. Now they learn *how to learn* in a laboratory. The emphasis is on the why rather than the how."

At Minnesota, Associate Dean Frank Verbrugge of the Institute of Technology, which includes the schools of architecture, chemistry, physics, mines and metallurgy as well as the College of Engineering, told much the same story: "Our course in mechanics and materials, for instance, now is a basic analytical course. There's no more materials testing, and you couldn't find an internal combustion engine on the place. Electrical testing has been replaced by work on electric and electronic circuits."

In mathematics no less than in science, the advance in knowledge in recent years has led to the need for sharp reappraisal of what shall be taught, and how. The most exciting thing that has happened, of course, is the development of high-speed computers. Opening as they do the possibility of much more advanced and intensive scientific research—simply because a researcher can now accomplish in minutes computations that might previously have taken years—they are of prime importance to the engineer.

In January 1962 a committee of the Mathematical Association of America issued a report called *Recommendations on the Undergraduate Mathematics Program for Engineers and Physicists*. The committee, which had as its chairman R. Creighton Buck of the Land-Grant University of Wisconsin and as its executive director Robert J. Wisner of MSUO, drew its findings from extensive conferences with mathematicians, physicists, and engineers, including a formal Conference on the Engineering Curriculum, which it had sponsored in 1961, with the American Society for Engineering Education.

In part it concluded that the electronic computer "is having its effect on every phase of science and technology, all the way from basic research to the production line. . . . It has, for one thing, moved some techniques from the abstract to the practical field. . . . Then too, computers have led people to tackle problems they would never have considered before. . . ."

This is aside from the rapidly increasing sophistication in theoretical mathematics (which allows people to think up tougher problems for the machines). It is aside, too, from curricular advances in secondary and even elementary schools which in a few years are expected to see almost every engineering and science-minded high school graduate in command of the mathematical insights now gained only after at least one year of college work.

In step with these developments, progressive engineering schools are offering, some requiring, courses in the use of digital computers. More precisely, they are training people in how to make use of them, not in how to connect the wires and plugs that make them click out the answers. Already Illinois requires all electrical and aeronautical engineering sophomores to take a course in "coding" or "programming" of computers, setting up the problems to be fed into the machines. "Ultimately," Everitt said, "this will be required of all our sophomores, but right now we don't have enough computers, or instructors, to do this."

Minnesota offers two elective undergraduate courses and a graduate course in the theory and programming of computers. MSUO, which acquired its first machine in early 1962, also plans to introduce coding work into its curriculum.

As a happy consequence of the elimination of many of the "hardware" and demonstration courses at these and other schools, there is now room for more work in the liberal arts, social sciences, and humanities, the second goal of thoughtful engineering leaders.

At MSUO, for example, engineering proper accounts for about 30 per cent of the engineering curriculum, and science and mathematics for about the same, leaving a whopping 40 per cent for liberal arts.

"Forty percent liberal arts is a little over twice the national average for engineering curricula," Hammerle conceded, "and I suspect that this may be too high. I believe it should be more than the national average—that the engineer should know something about music, something about China—but I don't know the percentage that would be proper."

At both Minnesota and Illinois, commitment to liberal arts for engineers is mirrored as brilliantly as at MSUO. Minnesota began a thoroughgoing overhaul of the curriculum of its Institute of Technology immediately after World War II and in 1949 installed a five-year program in most sequences. "One of the motives," Verbrugge emphasized, was to allow greater requirements in the humanities, social sciences and liberal arts. Probably the one important thing about a Land-Grant institution in this respect is that the major liberal arts program and the engineering program are on the same campus. What this means is that we can insist that our students take liberal arts right in the Liberal Arts College.

It was at our request, five years ago, that a special freshman English class for engineering students was dropped. They now must take regular freshman English, and everyone is very happy about it. The Liberal Arts College has discovered that the engineering student does have an interest in the humanities.

Illinois not only has given the social sciences and humanities new emphasis as electives in recent years, at the expense of such things as accounting, but has tackled the problem farther down, at the high school level. It instituted a joint study of its entrance requirements by the university's Committee on School-University Relations and the Illinois Association of Secondary School Principals. The outcome was that, effective in September 1963, engineering entrance requirements were stiffly upgraded, with new emphasis on nonscientific subjects. Two units of a foreign language were required, and a third recommended, and an additional year of English was recommended over the existing three-year requirement.

The proposal met strong opposition from many of the technical high schools in the state, but Everitt and his colleagues stuck by their guns, with the consequence, Everitt observed with a chuckle, that "the liberal arts college is now following our lead."

The forces which have remolded undergraduate engineering education have had their impact on graduate education as well. Moreover, as a consequence of the vast increase in the body of engineering and scientific knowledge, and of the stress which is being laid on development of engineering leaders, more and more engineering students feel it is imperative to go on for advanced work.

In the spring of 1951, all engineering schools in the country, public and private, conferred about 42,000 bachelor's degrees, 5,000 master's degrees, and 600 Ph.D.'s. In the spring of 1961 they conferred approximately 32,000 bachelor's degrees, 8,000 master's degrees, and nearly 1,000 Ph.D.'s. Granted that the total number of all degrees declined, the important thing is that Ph.D. degrees in engineering went from about one-eighth of the total in 1951 to almost one-fourth in 1961.

That Land-Grant engineering schools did their share is demonstrated by the following tabulation by the U.S. Office of Education for the seven-year period 1954-60 inclusive, showing the six universities (Land-Grant institutions are starred) which were top producers of Ph.D.'s in engineering:

*Massachusetts Institute of Technology	569
*University of Illinois	303
University of Michigan	245
*Purdue University (Indiana)	244
Stanford University	204
*University of Wisconsin	158

Even discounting the unique situation of MIT, noted previously, the Land-Grant record is impressive.

While all, or virtually all, Ph.D.'s are awarded after full-time, on-campus work, some bachelor's and master's degrees are awarded for evening or other part-time study under general extension. In view of the continual burgeoning of engineering knowledge, coupled with the practical fact that many working engineers simply cannot break away to take full-time university work, extension courses are assuming an ever-increasing importance.

President Richard G. Folsom of Rensselaer Polytechnic Institute, who evaluated Land-Grant engineering extension work in a paper at Kansas City, put it this way: "Recent studies show that the average man works 43 years during his lifetime. Unless he is engaged in some form of self-education or continuing education, the practicing professional engineer who works his average span will be almost completely outdated for more than a half of his working life."

Folsom cited statistics showing that in the 1960-61 academic year 14 Land-Grant universities enrolled 963 evening students working on master's degrees and four enrolled 28 working on the Ph.D. This compared to 10 Land-Grant institutions enrolling 562 M.A. candidates in evening classes in 1958-59 and two enrolling 33 doctoral candidates. Although this represents an increase from 595 to 991 in total numbers of advanced students, Folsom could only conclude that "we are discussing a potential, rather than a large and thriving operation."

Leading in evening enrollment were Wisconsin with 241 master's candidates, Connecticut with 176 master's and 13 Ph.D. candidates, Purdue with 188 master's, Ohio State with 85, and Delaware with 66 seeking their master's and nine their doctor's degrees.

One handicap under which most Land-Grant universities operate with respect to on-campus engineering extension work, or any extension work, is that they are not usually located in major industrial cities, where engineers in need of advanced work are usually centered. This may be overcome if the university is able to establish a branch of some sort in an industrial area, but this is not always feasible. Conceding the difficulties, Folsom nonetheless emphatically stated:

Graduate instruction holds the same relative importance in engineering education as undergraduate instruction did at the time of the establishment of the [Morrill] Act. Unfortunately, this is not sufficiently recognized and understood by many academic administrators nor by state governments. . . .

The longest step forward that can be made at the present time in engineering instruction by Land-Grant colleges is the active support of graduate instruction and research. In such a program the graduate extension activities will become increasingly important, and they must be included as a vital element in any long-range planning for an outstanding Land-Grant college or state university.

Land-Grant universities have always been in the forefront of engineering research, as even a partial listing of their contributions—the television tube, the transistor, basic work on metal fatigue which greatly increased the life of railroad wheels and tracks—will demonstrate.

In general, the research carried on at engineering colleges is like all scientific research in that it is either basic or applied. In the case of engineering particularly, however, there is frequently another differentiation: some technological research is carried on as a service-type function, often under a government contract, almost detached from the university itself, while other research involves students as part of their education.

Carl C. Chambers, vice president of the University of Pennsylvania, who served as outside evaluator of engineering research, posed the issue in his report at Kansas City. After first noting that "engineering research . . . has been undertaken by Land-Grant institutions in a widely varying degree, ranging from almost insignificant effort in certain institutions to a tremendous effort at the Massachusetts Institute of Technology," Chambers emphasized:

Research is essential to the process known as "university education." While it is true that *training,* even vocational training, does not necessarily require a climate of inquiry, education in the sense of engineering education demands such a climate of scholarship. The term "engineering research" has come to mean the activities of the faculty and of the student body which provide this climate. . . . It contributes little to the education of the students to have research conducted on one side of the campus by one group of faculty members and to have instruction given on the other side by a separate group.

An important instrument available for bringing the student into research is the engineering experiment station that is found in some states. Chambers cited Oklahoma State University as one institution where the experiment station has "cooperated closely with the teaching activity," a practice which he characterized as valuable also because "without research or other experience on the frontiers of engineering, teachers become incompetent."

Another university where the engineering experiment station is importantly "wired in" with teaching is the University of Illinois. "Along with the growth in graduate work, principally since 1945," said Ross J. Martin, director of the Illinois station, during the visit there, "we have carried on a dynamic research program. About a fourth of the students here are graduate students. Our research budget is over twice as much as our instructional budget, and it is built primarily around our graduate work. We just don't have a lot of research without student involvement. In this respect we differ from Argonne Center and Project Lincoln."

Argonne Center and Project Lincoln are large research activities at the University of Chicago and MIT, respectively, which were organized to meet special national defense purposes. They draw heavily on university faculty as staff members, and thus have done much to promote the "interdisciplinary" approach to research which is gaining increasing recognition as essential in modern science—engineers, biologists, and physicists working together on an aerospace project, for instance. However, they are not closely related to the educational activities of their parent institutions. Chambers did not deny the need for such research establishments, or belittle their accomplishments. But he expressed the strong caution in his paper that although "the institution may reap some public recognition because of the work of such laboratories [he named the Cornell Aeronautical Laboratory as another example], they should not be viewed . . . as integral with the main function of the university."

As a norm, Chambers proposed that about half the time of an engineering faculty as a whole should be devoted to teaching during the academic year, with the rest of the time over the entire 12 months devoted to research, thesis guidance, and other research-related activities. Only when research demands by a school's constituency reach the point where they cannot be met within this ratio, he held, should an independent laboratory be set up.

So far, Chambers continued, although a few Land-Grant

institutions may have exceeded this "to the detriment of the educational program," in most of them "too much of their faculty time is devoted to teaching and too little to research." One reason, he said, was that "for the past several decades the resources of the Land-Grant institutions were stressed to the limit to engage teachers of engineering courses without requiring research interest and activity."

As of now, Chambers was "impressed with the desirable balance which seems to have been attained in the University of Illinois," a balance which he expected to become more widespread since "recently many Land-Grant schools have adopted faculty recruitment principles which will improve the scholarship of the faculty as the later appointees become predominant." He observed, however, that up to now "the private institutions have been ahead of the Land-Grant institutions in many instances in this respect."

The nature and scope of engineering research has changed in recent years as well as the amount of it and methods of carrying it on. Again, while some colleges have responded well to modern demands, it is plain that most have not. The foreword to the Engineers Joint Council report, *The Nation's Engineering Research Needs*, states that one of the reasons for undertaking the study was "concern over the apparent rigidity of U.S. institutions associated with engineering," including engineering schools, "which are often slow to recognize and respond to new challenges and opportunities arising from the changing needs of society."

One instance of quick recognition and response to these new challenges is Minnesota's Institute of Technology. As Verbrugge summarized it:

Our research has gone very much in the direction of applying scientific principles to the engineering art. It is no longer a matter of the improvement of the engineering art as an art. We are probably doing 100 times as much research as we did before the war, and it is all basic research, under direct grants and contracts, rather than sub-contract work on applications.

In aeronautical engineering, for example, we are studying boundary layer problems of aerfoils, the heat transfer across this layer, rather than designing an aerfoil. In metallurgy we go into the fundamental phenomena of crystalline defects and their relationship to microscopic properties of metals rather than fabricate a metal.

For all the developing emphasis on engineering science, and educating a man for the job he will hold "20 years from now," realistic engineering educators concede that there is still need for the graduate who will go right to work in an applied field. As Hammerle at MSUO remarked: "We don't claim that ours is the only way to teach engineering, but just that somebody ought to be doing it. We need the traditional kind of engineering too."

But for those who are exposed to an engineering science curriculum, and can handle it, how does it pay off? Perhaps the words of a young MSUO student, taking a few hours off from his vacation job in a nearby auto plant, provide the best kind of answer: "Many men in my department with college engineering degrees are doing the same thing as those who have worked their way up without going to college. The college training those men got—traditional engineering education—they might as well not have had."

CHAPTER THIRTEEN

Education of Teachers

"To a layman," observed Lawrence D. Haskew, " 'Land-Grant' is almost synonymous with 'at the grass roots.' He expects direct service to be the trademark of institutions with this name. He thinks the campus climate almost forces such involvement."

In few areas of Land-Grant endeavor can this be more truly said than in that of service to public schools, and the education of teachers, the area in which Haskew, former dean of education and now vice chancellor at the University of Texas, served as outside evaluator at Kansas City.

A veteran in his field, Haskew nevertheless confessed at the outset of his paper that he was frankly astonished not to find "some unique flavors to teacher education in Land-Grant institutions." Teacher education, he said, "appears to be capsuled within institutional individuality rather than within the name of an association to which an institution belongs."

The fact that all the institutions concerned do belong to an association, however—the Association of State Universities and Land-Grant Colleges—gave Haskew an excellent springboard in that he could compare their accomplishments in all aspects of teacher education with their record in the education of teachers in just two fields, agriculture and home economics.

"I submit," he said, "that no subjects have ever been better taught in American high schools than the subjects of agriculture and homemaking; that no contingent of teachers have ever equalled the teachers of agriculture and homemaking in command of their specialized subject matter; that no more effective curricula . . . have been designed than in those two fields. . . . This story, one of the brightest in American education, is written by Land-Grant colleges and universities."

Although expressing uneasiness that "the sense of crusading, of inventive research does not come through now as one talks to agriculture and homemaking educators" as it seemed to him it did in the past, and inquiring whether "the patterns evolved . . . should be imitated in the 1960s," Haskew declared "the successes achieved warrant strong efforts toward emulation."

Sessions of the Teacher Education Division at the Centennial Convocation opened with a report by Dean Lindley J. Stiles of the University of Wisconsin, who had surveyed all Land-Grant institutions and analyzed the status of their teacher education as of June 1961.

Of the 139,000 qualified teachers graduated from all institutions of higher learning with teacher training programs, Stiles noted, 17,010—or 13.1 per cent—were graduated from 66 Land-Grant institutions. Since Land-Grant colleges and universities represent only 5.4 per cent of all such institutions, this meant that they did more than twice their proportionate share during the 1961-62 year.

Predictably, the Land-Grant institutions turned out 59.3 per cent of the teachers of agriculture and a high percentage—25.8—of the teachers of home economics. Yet, despite this weighting influence, Stiles's figures showed, "in all fields the percentages of teachers produced by Land-Grant institutions exceed the relative share of the nation's teachers that these colleges and universities might be expected to produce." To the possible astonishment of some who still think of the Land-Grant institutions as "cow colleges," it may be reported that next in order behind teachers of agriculture and home economics were teachers of music and art, of whom 19.5 per cent and 17.3 per cent, respectively, were Land-Grant products.

At the graduate level, Dean Stiles found that 62 of the Land-Grant institutions offer work leading to the master's degree and that 42 of these also offer the doctorate. In 1961-62 only 55 of these actually awarded such degrees. Even so, they accounted for some 15 per cent of the master's degrees and for more than 34 per cent of all the doctorates—doctor of education or doctor of philosophy in education—awarded by all institutions offering teacher education. The figures were: 3,997 M.A.'s, 241 Ed.D.'s, and 239 Ph.D.'s.

It was within this framework that Haskew assessed the effectiveness of teacher training in the Land-Grant system; many of his conclusions were based on another questionnaire circulated especially for his study. Haskew began by setting up five criteria:

1. *Commitment*—as indicated by, for one thing, "extra efforts to provide rich academic resources for teachers, for careful design in programs followed by teachers-to-be."

2. *Productive Attention*—"meaningful controls of the quality of what is offered and what is done, controls which steadily replace mediocrity with adequacy defined in language of modern needs and modern possibilities."

3. *Sensitivity*—"to the meaning of sound and essential academic attainment . . . to the real needs of young students . . . to the demands placed upon teachers, the live, practical, real necessities generated by entering a classroom and closing the door."

4. *Tooling*—"the first essential is acquiring, holding and unleashing faculty members of requisite competence, but it is a matter of men, *and* machines, *and* materials, each assisting in the maximum exploitation of the other."

5. *Pioneering*—"contributions to educational research, to the body of fact which simply must replace folklore as the prime reliance for educational advancement in this century."

After first cautioning that consideration should be given to the wide range in size among Land-Grant institutions—The Ohio State University enrolled more than 5,000 students in teacher education in 1960-61, and North Dakota State University only 60—Haskew proceeded to match the Land-Grant effort in teacher education point by point with his criteria, beginning with commitment. "Relatively," he said, "the combined commitment of these 66 institutions to teacher education is probably as great as that in any other set of 66 institutions selected at random."

But, he immediately added: "Absolutely, the composite picture resembles one of fairly good-natured compliance much more than it does one of resolute pursuit. . . . It is not that teacher education is treated in niggardly fashion or is unwelcome or even disregarded. It is that it leads a sort of old war-horse existence, counted on to pull a big part of the load but seldom entered in the big races."

Naturally, there are extremes of good and bad within any composite picture. Haskew hastened to point out, in fact: "Here is one institution which . . . is placing nearly one-fourth of its venture capital for acquisition of top-flight faculty members at the disposal of its teacher education people. Another has made the needs of teacher education a prominent reason for strengthening its natural science departments. Another has allocated a large proportion of its research funds to investigations in learning. . . ." In all, Haskew said he would put 10 Land-Grant institutions "far out on the commitment end of the scale."

Nevertheless, he continued, "the impression of willing compliance remains the dominant one. . . . I would opine that at least one-half of the members of the association have demonstrated more commitment to other objectives than they have to the objectives of teacher education."

(Although no one challenged Haskew on this statement, it might have been pointed out—in this and other connections—that in some states responsibility for teacher education is placed primarily on other colleges or universities, under coordinated plans through which various institutions emphasize various fields. The same might be said of private institutions—not every nonpublic university is outstanding in every area.)

Turning to his second criterion, productive attention, Haskew took as models "the kind of institutions which, because of design and energy and resources and perspiration, are turning out results which are noteworthy when checked against the needs which exist." "Noteworthy" he characterized as having three dimensions: quantity, scope, and quality.

On the first score, quantity, he readily conceded that "the Land-Grant institutions of this country are getting highly significant results," at least as far as production of educational workers—teachers and others—is concerned.

As respects quantity in other types of educational endeavor, however, he found the story somewhat less encouraging. "The volume of direct service to school systems is large and impressive," he said. "Special in-service offerings [to improve teacher competence] abound. Publications and conferences and cooperative projects are numerous. Participation in state or nationwide school improvement projects is common." But, although he concluded that "the total volume of direct service must be accorded significant status," he estimated that "12 universities account for two-thirds of the total direct service volume."

In research, experimentation, and demonstration in education, said Haskew—whose congenital saltiness was one of the delights of the whole Convocation—the Land-Grant institutions "produce a volume which stands out like a grey cat in a coal mine."

Explaining, he continued: "They spent more than $425,-000,000 on organized research in 1958-59. It is difficult to trace more than $5,000,000 of it into education. . . . One institution reported an expenditure above $700,000; five others were over the quarter-million mark. They make the cat grey instead of completely black."

What is being done in experimentation and demonstration, he added, does not enhance this part of the picture much. "True," he said, "several institutions operate elementary and secondary schools under the banners of 'demonstration' or 'laboratory,' but it's a pity to visit the classrooms in those schools and so frequently have one's illusions shattered."

Having said all this, however, Haskew made it clear that in his opinion no other segment of higher education was doing much better in research, experimentation, or demonstration—"The environment is black, and this makes the Land-Grant cat at least distinguishable." He estimated that half of the work being done in these three phases of education might well be going forward in Land-Grant institutions.

Turning next to scope, the second element in his examination of productive attention, Haskew found that "in programs for students, total scope is impressive." Of 19 fields of teaching specialization listed by the U.S. Office of Education as leading to the bachelor's degree, his survey showed, some Land-Grant institution produces graduates in every one, with each of eight found in more than half of them.

And, he continued, in a reflection of Stiles's findings, "the thrust of these institutions into second-level [master's] and doctorate work in education is remarkable, as is their rate of spread into fields of graduate specialization."

One thing that bothered Haskew, however, in connection with production of educational personnel, was "when scope ceases to be blessing and becomes bane":

> The scope of student education for teaching provided in these institutions has certainly reached the blessing stage. One gets a strong impression that in some instances it has passed into bane at the advanced degree levels.
>
> Faculty versatility and capacity to work must be truly phenomenal in some institutions, or else the specialties offered are suspiciously thin. . . . Graduate degree programs in school administration are much more numerous than the demand for

employment warrants and, on the surface at least, more wide-spread than institutional resources justify.

Haskew found the scope of off-campus services to be "wide in composite but extremely narrow in many institutions." Yet, he conceded, "some of the institutions with the narrowest range of services may be exceptionally wise. They may have chosen to do a little well, to avoid duplication of what other institutions, state agencies and federal organizations are in position to do better."

The last item which Haskew examined from the point of view of scope was research and experimentation, which he described as "pitifully narrow, in spite of encouraging developments at four or five large state universities." Using 15 "new" ideas in education to make a sample check, he found that each was being tried by two to 10 Land-Grant colleges of education, with 10 other ideas being explored experimentally by one or more. "However," he reported, "one can take 40 of the institutions and get no hint of organized, planned experimental endeavours."

Finally, in his appraisal of productive attention, Haskew looked at the matter of quality, at four aspects in particular: faculty recruitment practices, curriculum revision, academic standards, and the use of new procedures.

With respect to faculty recruitment he reported "some pictures of extraordinary efforts to get just the man or woman needed" not only by eminent state universities "but also occasionally from smaller schools." He also reported pictures of "easy expectations, choosing from those who apply." This, he conceded, may be "simply gracious bowing to the inevitable" in view of the well-known general shortage of teachers at all levels. Nevertheless, he added, there seems to be "more grace than gumption."

Curricular revision, Haskew admitted, "does not necessarily signify improvement," but "it does disclose that some type of yeast is working." Of the Land-Grant system as a whole, he found: "Recasting of any part of the undergraduate curriculum is a unique phenomenon. Some graduate programs have undergone sweeping change, it is reported. However, the situation with regard to [graduate work in] educational administration appears all too typical. Twenty-nine of these institutions offer such programs; in only seven could any real change be documented."

One aspect of curriculum revision in teachers colleges which Haskew did not touch upon was the fact that numerous Land-Grant institutions have instituted university-wide curricular changes which have perforce resulted in changes in their teachers colleges. The "basic colleges" at Michigan State University and the University of Florida are two examples; another of a slightly different sort is the system of comprehensive courses at Kansas State University. The purpose of both plans is to ensure that every university student gets a specified core of academic work. It might also be pointed out that a great many of the Ford Foundation grants to improve teacher education have been to Land-Grant colleges and universities, a substantial number of them to smaller institutions.

With reference to academic standards, Haskew found that most institutions report they are "tightening up, exacting higher attainments than were required a few years ago. . . . At least one-fourth have raised admission hurdles to be cleared by freshmen. Very few have done so for admission to graduate study, and if the general movement of academic stiffening has entered the graduate field it hides itself well." Haskew conceded that such evidence "does not get at the essence of academic standards, the real meat that must be chewed and digested, the real stretching of mind and of abilities-to-do which are expected."

New procedures were investigated by Haskew, "again, not because new is a magic word but because it does demonstrate attention and interest." He reported "some highly encouraging inventions" and went on to say: "One hears references to improvements in student teaching, improvements in English writing laboratories, improved demonstrations in natural sciences, extensive developments in individual study, and so on. Then, one asks employers what they think is happening to the quality of the beginning teachers. The few institutions that have told about such inquiries report universally that employers say that today's beginners are markedly superior to those of a decade or so ago." One might be quite encouraged, he continued, "if it were not for one fact. Genuine, well-tooled attempts to evaluate the quality of what is being done are almost non-existent."

Haskew then turned to his next criterion, sensitivity. Again he found a great range, "from institutions whose chief motive power is inertia—they are fairly well satisfied that they are trying to do the right thing—to those which are deriving acceleration from the stimulations of their environment. . . . Take 15 of these institutions and you get an impression of dynamic, even frenetic, response. Take 66 and the scene is alive but only gently kicking."

The area in which Haskew found most Land-Grant teachers colleges particularly lacking in sensitivity was that of the needs and potentialities of their students. "The normal classroom attitude," he said, "is still one of take it or leave it. Far more organized faculty attention seems to be devoted to enacting requirements for enforced withdrawal than to procedures for reinforced instruction."

On the other hand, he found sensitivity to what is happening in schools at a very high level.

"These institutions," he commented, "almost without exception convey an impression of being abreast of the times. They may be too responsive to fads and gadgetry [but] many of them are in the vanguard of efforts to reconstitute subject content in physics, mathematics, biology, English."

Outstanding examples of secondary school curriculum improvement which might be cited as the work of Land-Grant institutions, whether through colleges of education or other divisions, are the new courses in physical sciences developed at MIT and California and the mathematics courses pioneered at Illinois.

On sensitivity to "the deeper aspects of societal and

educational change" and to research directed at solving educational problems, Haskew was less optimistic. "Few institutions reflect any deep awareness of fundamental issues at stake in guiding pupils to manage their lives in the 20th century," he observed with regard to the former point, adding by way of example: "A few voices are raised about the fundamental problems of human communication in literate but lonely crowds, but most institutions content themselves with offering workshops on how to teach rapid reading."

With reference to research on fundamental educational problems, Haskew reported that "the void in these institutions is a black one." He quoted one university administrator as saying: "We'll give our faculty in education as much research backing as they ask for. They do not ask for any."

One dean of education who certainly would meet Haskew's standards for sensitivity in research is W. K. Beggs of the University of Nebraska. In a Convocation paper on "Teacher Education in the Land-Grant Institutions of Tomorrow," Beggs told his fellow deans:

Research will be the master satellite. Unless we choose to go on in a "catch as catch can" atmosphere indefinitely, a major portion of our resources and of our effort must be devoted to plain hard-nosed experimentation based on research. The media, the team, programs, and systems could become the tail that wags the dog unless research shows the ways in which they can be best used. Further exploration of the nature of learning, and of the learning environment is an urgent need.

Equally important is the adaptation of research findings in other fields to the needs of education. No discovery relating to human behavior, to learning environment, or to human growth can be overlooked, and the whole complex must be redesigned to improve what a teacher does, how it is done and to evaluate the results that accrue from doing it.

Haskew, in summarizing his findings on sensitivity of Land-Grant schools of teacher education, concluded that all in all, "against a background of all higher education institutions as known to this observer, their sensitivity stands out with gratifying sharpness. Against a background of what is possible and desirable, gratification is diminished."

Proceeding to the question of tooling, Haskew took up first what he considered the Land-Grant institutions' weakest aspect under this heading—curriculum. Examining a random 20 teachers college catalogs, he had concluded that the " 'broad background in the basic fields of human knowledge' so bravely set forth as the *sine qua non* of becoming a teacher is typically tooled up with a potpourri of selections from introductory courses in this and that to reach a cash-register total." In only 16 of these catalogs did he find, for example, any requirement for study of expository writing beyond freshman composition—"Most just sent the student down a cafeteria line."

Student teaching he characterized as a glaring example of a program conducted "on a lick-and-promise basis . . . in all too many institutions." Frequently, he said, there may be "one college supervisor for 30 to 40 students, inadequate cooperating centers, very little refinement of simple trial-and-error processes."

On tooling of research, he was a little more encouraged. While "matters investigated are seldom of great moment or complexity," he reported, "design is increasingly sophisticated; statistical tools are being employed wisely . . . theory is being talked about to notable degree."

In tooling through materials and facilities, again, he found much to be desired. Many institutions afford a rich array of books, charts, sound movies, and the like, he reported, but the median "would not be creditable, speaking relatively, to a good junior high school." As for facilities, he summarized the general situation—again noting encouraging exceptions—by quoting a university president who returned his questionnaire form with the comment: "Teacher education has as good facilities as anyone else on this campus—except, of course, those divisions such as natural sciences and medicine which must have good equipment to do their work."

The final aspect of tooling, as Haskew explored it, was faculty and staff. Sensing that he may have downgraded teachers college faculties to an undue extent in earlier comments, he said at this point: "To counter over-generalization . . . let me say that on my personal list of top scholars in teacher education at least 40 per cent of the names are drawn from member institutions in this association." Even so, he added, "a norm of expertness is not yet in evidence" in the Land-Grant institutions.

Concluding his evaluation, Haskew examined the pioneering that is going on in Land-Grant teacher education. "Fresh, revolutionary, provocative points of view about the nature of universal education and, hence, the nature of teacher education, are the cockleburs under the saddle blanket which instill liveliness," he said. "Are these institutions growing any cockleburs?" Answering his own question, he declared:

They have made "break throughs." They have attracted outside grants for experimental programs, have received more than their normal share of grants from the pittances the federal government makes available for research in education, have launched pioneering curriculum endeavors and direct-service enterprises with their own resources.

Thus, we can call them pioneers. In the company of all leading universities, however, their volume of pioneering does not appear quite so large. The five best of them can hold up their heads in any company, the next 10 are convincingly overshadowed although definitely in the "show" category, and only a few of the remainder join the also-rans.

Valued against the yardstick of what ought to be, what is needed, what is possible, perhaps all are found wanting. Some are definitely in the company of the best pioneers, but the best is none too good.

Having finished his evaluation, Haskew set forth four challenges for the Land-Grant teacher-training schools. The first was for what he called "evangelism." He explained in these words:

One of the things America needs most is a demonstration of what would happen if one public university of high caliber really committed itself to teacher education for one decade. . . . Here is where the pace will be set. Here is where the numerical problem will be solved if it is to be solved. Here is where the bellwether brainpower needed for school classrooms will be found. Here is where the real tone of the American school system in the 1970s will be created. . . . The challenge is that some deans and some professors and some alumni and some other power figures connected with a single institution set themselves to this task.

Haskew's second challenge was to "a quest—a ceaseless, determined, hard-nosed quest for quality." This "is a challenge to small institutions. . . . It is a challenge to the largest, as well as the very best, institutions represented in this association; they should have gone, by now, beyond the need for symbolical performances and be ready to embrace real quality defined in terms of changes produced."

The third challenge was "a call to inquiry—to research, experimentation, fact-finding, philosophical rumination. . . ."

Lastly, Haskew called anew for more pioneering. "Pioneering is a disciplined undertaking," he told his listeners in measured phrases. "The challenge is not to activity but to exploration, and exploration is bought with a price. The price of planning. The price of assembling resources. The price of organizing an expedition. The price of thoughtful forecasting. The price of evaluating. And, over and over again, the price of plain hard work, but work with transcendent zest and freshness to it."

CHAPTER FOURTEEN

Military Instruction

"Just what we would have done in the early phases of our mobilization and training without these men I do not know. I do know that our plans would have had to be greatly curtailed and the cessation of hostilities on the European front would have been delayed accordingly."

The speaker was General George C. Marshall, World War II chief of staff of the Army, and "these men" were some 100,000 Army Reserve officers trained on college campuses during prewar years in the Army Reserve Officers Training Corps—the ROTC. The Army estimated that their availability in the war-shadowed summer of 1940 enabled it to increase its active strength fivefold within a year. In 1944 a check of five veteran divisions disclosed that three-fourths of their captains and majors were ROTC graduates.

More than half of the ROTC-trained officers who served in World War II received their training at Land-Grant institutions—indisputable evidence that these colleges and universities had honored to the fullest, as they had in the Spanish-American War and World War I, their obligation under the Morrill Act to provide instruction in "military tactics." Indisputable evidence of this, also, was the distinguished record of some 2,000 Naval Reserve officers who had received their training under Naval ROTC.

Although there is no question that the Land-Grant system will continue to honor this obligation, it is an unhappy fact that its relationships with the armed services steadily deteriorated after the end of World War II and only in the early 1960's were beginning to show an uncertain improvement.

The roots of this deterioration went back to the time of the war itself, and even earlier, but before exploring them it may be well, in the interest of a clear understanding of the question, to dispose of two common misconceptions, both inherent in the frequently heard statement that "every boy who goes to a Land-Grant college has to take ROTC."

The fact is that the only requirement under federal law is that Land-Grant institutions *offer* military instruction. It is not compulsory under federal law, and it need not be conducted through the government-sponsored ROTC.

Actually, 61 Land-Grant colleges and universities do handle military training through Army, Navy, or Air Force ROTC, and at 47 of these a basic two-year course is compulsory, with advanced training elective. Other Land-Grant institutions provide training through "local" cadet corps, as indeed all of them did before ROTC was set up in 1916 as part of the Army's World War I mobilization plan. At three of these, basic training is compulsory.

Table IV shows which Land-Grant institutions had ROTC units at the opening of the 1962-63 academic year, what kinds of units they had—Army, Navy, or Air Force— and whether basic training was compulsory or elective.

TABLE IV. *ROTC Units at Land-Grant Colleges and Universities, August 1962* [a]

State	Land-Grant Institution
Alabama	Auburn University—Army, Navy, Air Force
	Alabama Agricultural and Mechanical College (none)
Alaska	University of Alaska—Army

[a] Source: Advisory Panel on ROTC Affairs, Reserve Forces Policy Board.

State	Land-Grant Institution
Arizona	University of Arizona—Army, Air Force
Arkansas	University of Arkansas—Army, Air Force
	Agricultural, Mechanical and Normal College (none)
California	UNIVERSITY OF CALIFORNIA ^b—Army, Navy, Air Force
Colorado	COLORADO STATE UNIVERSITY—Army, Air Force
Connecticut	UNIVERSITY OF CONNECTICUT—Army, Air Force
Delaware	University of Delaware—Army
	Delaware State College (none)
Florida	University of Florida—Army, Air Force
	Florida Agricultural and Mechanical University—Army
Georgia	University of Georgia—Army, Air Force
	Fort Valley State College (none)
Hawaii	University of Hawaii—Army, Air Force
Idaho	* University of Idaho ^c—Army, Navy, Air Force
Illinois	University of Illinois—Army, Navy, Air Force
Indiana	Purdue University—Army, Navy, Air Force
Iowa	IOWA STATE UNIVERSITY—Army, Navy, Air Force
Kansas	Kansas State University—Army, Air Force
Kentucky	University of Kentucky—Army, Air Force
	Kentucky State College (none)
Louisiana	Louisiana State University—Army, Air Force
	Southern University—Army
Maine	* University of Maine—Army
Maryland	University of Maryland—Air Force
	Maryland State College—Air Force
Massachusetts	* University of Massachusetts—Army, Air Force
	MASSACHUSETTS INSTITUTE OF TECHNOLOGY—Army, Navy, Air Force
Michigan	* Michigan State University—Army, Air Force
Minnesota	UNIVERSITY OF MINNESOTA—Army, Navy, Air Force
Mississippi	Mississippi State University—Army, Air Force
	Alcorn Agricultural and Mechanical College (none)

^b Capital letters indicate ROTC is elective.
^c Asterisk indicates ROTC becomes elective in fall of 1963.

State	Land-Grant Institution
Missouri	University of Missouri—Army, Navy, Air Force
	Lincoln University—Army
Montana	Montana State College—Army, Air Force
Nebraska	University of Nebraska—Army, Navy, Air Force
Nevada	University of Nevada—Army
New Hampshire	University of New Hampshire—Army, Air Force
New Jersey	RUTGERS UNIVERSITY—Army, Air Force
New Mexico	New Mexico State University—Army, Air Force
New York	CORNELL UNIVERSITY—Army, Navy, Air Force
North Carolina	North Carolina State College—Army, Air Force
	Agricultural and Technical College of North Carolina—Army, Air Force
North Dakota	North Dakota State University—Army, Air Force
Ohio	OHIO STATE UNIVERSITY—Army, Navy, Air Force
Oklahoma	Oklahoma State University—Army, Air Force
	Langston University (none)
Oregon	OREGON STATE UNIVERSITY—Army, Navy, Air Force
Pennsylvania	Pennsylvania State University—Army, Navy, Air Force
Puerto Rico	UNIVERSITY OF PUERTO RICO—Army, Air Force
Rhode Island	University of Rhode Island—Army
South Carolina	Clemson Agricultural College—Army, Air Force
	South Carolina State College—Army
South Dakota	South Dakota State College—Army, Air Force
Tennessee	Tennessee Agricultural and Industrial State University—Air Force
	University of Tennessee—Army, Air Force
Texas	Agricultural and Mechanical College of Texas—Army, Air Force
	Prairie View Agricultural and Mechanical College—Army
Utah	UTAH STATE UNIVERSITY—Army, Air Force
Vermont	University of Vermont—Army
Virginia	Virginia Polytechnic Institute—Army, Air Force
	Virginia State College—Army
Washington	WASHINGTON STATE UNIVERSITY—Army, Air Force
West Virginia	West Virginia University—Army, Air Force

State	Land-Grant Institution
Wisconsin	UNIVERSITY OF WISCONSIN—Army, Navy, Air Force
Wyoming	University of Wyoming—Army, Air Force

Totals: compulsory, 47
elective, 14
no ROTC, 7 [d]

[d] Among those institutions which have non-ROTC cadet corps, training is compulsory at Fort Valley (Ga.) State College, Alcorn (Miss.) Agricultural and Mechanical College, and Langston (Okla.) University.

A recapitulation of this table shows that: 15 institutions had Army, Navy, and Air Force units, seven of them on a compulsory basis, of which one planned to shift to elective basis in the fall of 1963; 31 had Army and Air Force units, 25 compulsory but with two of these also to shift to elective basis in the fall of 1963; 12 had Army units only, all compulsory but with one to become elective in the fall of 1963; 3 had Air Force units only, also all compulsory.

Table V shows enrollment in all three types of ROTC at all U.S. colleges and universities, public and private, and at Land-Grant institutions alone at the end of the 1961-62 academic year, the number of units [1] at each, and percentage of Land-Grant enrollment to all enrollment.

From Table V it is apparent that the Land-Grant colleges and universities, which enroll about 19.5 per cent of all U.S. male college students, were doing more than twice their share—with 44.3 per cent of ROTC enrollees—in training future officers for the armed services.

It will surely be a long time, if ever, before the Land-Grant institutions do less than their share. Nevertheless, the fact that 14 of those with ROTC had placed it on an elective basis, with four more scheduled to go on that basis in the fall of 1963, is suggestive.

At one time ROTC was compulsory, under either state law or institutional regulation, at nearly every Land-Grant

[1] Some institutions had more than one kind of unit in the same service, for example an Army engineer unit *and* an infantry unit. Thus, there were 62 Army units at 58 Land-Grant institutions.

TABLE v. *ROTC Enrollment and Number of Units at All Institutions and at Land-Grant Institutions, Close of Academic Year 1961-62* [a]

| | All Institutions | | | | Land-Grant Institutions | | | | |
| | Enrollment | | | No. of Units | Enrollment | | | No. of Units | Per Cent Land-Grant Enrollment to All |
	Basic	Advanced	Total		Basic	Advanced	Total		
Army	129,650	25,712	155,362	232	55,088	9,048	64,136	62	41.0
Navy [b]	6,435	3,887	10,322	53	2,456	1,371	3,827	16	37.0
Air Force	82,010	5,989	87,999	172	44,570	3,035	47,605	49	55.0
Totals	218,095	35,588	253,683	457	102,114	13,454	115,568	127	44.3

[a] Sources: Army—Office of the Adjutant General; Navy—Bureau of Naval Personnel; Air Force—Directorate of Personnel Procurement and Training.

[b] Naval ROTC is not actually divided into basic and advanced sections but in order to permit comparison with the other services the Navy classified its enrollment in two groups, freshman-sophomore and junior-senior.

college and university. In the 1920's there was widespread sentiment against compulsory military training, and as a consequence of this three Land-Grant institutions, the universities of Minnesota and Wisconsin and North Dakota State College (now University) discontinued it. However, the latter two reinstated it just after World War II.

Thus, in all but one case, the 18 Land-Grant institutions which had placed ROTC on an elective basis by 1962, or announced plans to do so, had taken this step since World War II—in most cases, in fact, since 1957.

As World War II opened there were only two kinds of ROTC in the field, Army and Navy. Army ROTC had been a going concern since World War I. NROTC, as the Navy's training corps is known, had been started in 1926.

During World War II the Army closed down its ROTC program, relying instead on the Officer Candidate School system under which men were selected from the ranks for training in accelerated courses. The Navy continued its relatively small NROTC program but also set up its well-known V-12 operation, an on-campus officer training program, for the most part at institutions where NROTC was already established, but at others also.

Very soon after the end of the war the Navy obtained congressional approval for its "Holloway Plan," named after the then deputy chief of naval personnel, Rear Admiral James L. Holloway, Jr. This was and still is a four-year program, integrated with a regular educational program, which recommends it to college administrators, with students supported by scholarships.

In establishing the Holloway Plan, the Navy converted its strongest V-12 units into NROTC units and was soon riding on a fairly even keel. The Army, however, having lost continuity during the war, got off to a slow postwar start.

Meanwhile, another element had come into the ROTC situation—Air Force ROTC, or AFROTC. The Air Force had established an ROTC system in 1946, while it was still part of the Army. It was separated from the Army in 1948, with establishment of the Department of Defense, but it is still controlled by basic Army legislation. Consequently AFROTC operates under the same general rules as ROTC —being compulsory on the same campuses as Army ROTC where both have units, for example—even though the needs of the two services in terms of officers have increasingly diverged. Like the Army, the Air Force got off to a slow postwar start on ROTC.

When the Army and Air Force did get moving after the war, it was with tremendous expansion plans. They added many new ROTC units and each set goals of more than 25,000 new officers per year, to be commissioned on completion of their two-year advanced courses. Some of these were to be taken directly into service as regular officers, some were to go on extended active duty, some into the reserve with little or no active duty.

One apparent reason for the Army's and Air Force's burst of energy was the thought that passage of a universal military training (UMT) bill by Congress was sure to come soon and that they would need large numbers of officers for training duty as well as to staff the large reserve forces which would emerge from UMT. The UMT bill failed, however, and the Army and Air Force were saddled with ROTC organizations that were turning out more reserve officers than they could possibly use.

During the Korean war the Secretary of Defense ruled that neither Army nor Air Force ROTC could train or commission more officers than it needed for active duty.

After the Korean war the Air Force continued this active-duty policy for AFROTC. With the development of bigger planes and a new concept of air warfare, it needed fewer and fewer pilots and other flight-qualified officers. Its annual requirements, at one time set at over 25,000, tapered off to about 3,000, all to go on five-year tours of active duty.

The Army eventually got back to its traditional plan of

taking some new officers into the regular service, keeping some for extended active duty, and placing some immediately on reserve. Of the latter, all were subject to a two-year call-up, but as late as 1962 about half were called for only six months, then returned to reserve status. Army requirements for new officers were down to about 15,000 a year.

Even with reduction in requirements, however, neither the Army nor the Air Force had done anything to counteract the consequences of their great overestimates of needs. Neither had taken steps to eliminate nonproductive units, which meant lower quotas—and higher costs—for productive units. Moreover, under sharp criticism from the Bureau of the Budget for this earlier overexpansion, they had not moved in to some large new institutions which would be highly productive. Some of the burgeoning campuses of the University of California, for instance, have no ROTC.

A serious consequence of this high-cost, low-quota procedure was that it destroyed an understanding reached at the time the Navy's Holloway Plan went into effect, an agreement that the Defense Department would attempt to provide facilities—armories, necessary additional classrooms, and the like—for military training, or at least share the cost of them. From the beginning, the government had furnished uniforms and military equipment and had detailed officers to serve as instructors, but the universities had had to provide necessary space.

Heightening the universities' chagrin at this development was their growing dissatisfaction with the academic aspects of Army and Air Force ROTC, in contrast to their rather general acceptance of the Navy's plan, which was structured as an integral part of the university program.

By and large, the views of the university people were accurately reflected in an article written by former Secretary of the Army Elvis Stahr in May 1962.[2] Stahr, a gradu-

[2] In *Scabbard and Blade Journal*, official publication of the National Society of Scabbard and Blade.

ate of the Land-Grant University of Kentucky and a former president of Land-Grant West Virginia University, later left his government post to become president of Indiana University. In the course of discussing various ROTC problems, he wrote: "ROTC curriculums have been the target of a good deal of academic criticism in recent years. The critics have pointed out the real or apparent differences between education and training in purpose and method, and urged that ROTC instruction on campuses be limited to education only."

Stahr recognized also that there had been criticism—"much of it," he said, "unjustified"—of the quality of instruction given by officer professors of military science and their assistants. But, he continued:

Perhaps the greatest difficulty in this area has been that of shaping a common course of instruction to suit all types of schools participating in a service ROTC program. Flexibility in adjustment to local needs and advantages, and substitution of civilian courses and instruction wherever that is needed, have helped materially. The Army now permits institutions to substitute civilian-taught courses in psychology, political science and other subjects amounting to 120 class hours during the basic and advanced courses. To the maximum practicable extent, the trend has been to move purely military instruction and training from the colleges to the summer camps.

Despite such revisions in academic approach as Stahr cited, however, there remained an overriding exasperation among Land-Grant and other educators at the lack of a cohesive and coordinated policy on ROTC. The Navy had its four-year program. The Air Force for some years had been pushing for a two-year scholarship-supported program for juniors and seniors—eliminating basic training, which would be covered in summertime activity—to be followed by extensive active duty. One important value of a two-year scheme would be that it would make a place for the fast-increasing number of junior college graduates entering colleges and universities without any ROTC training. The Army, torn by continuing internal dispute among those who wanted to keep the old-style Army program, those who wanted something like the Air Force plan, and those who wanted something in between, had presented no new plan at all.

Along with all this was the question of compulsory versus elective military training, and the Department of Defense's attitude in the matter. Up until 1957 the services, although doing nothing to help the universities carry it out, had insisted that they wanted compulsory ROTC, and most of the universities—often at great financial strain—had respected this expressed wish. Then hints began to emanate from the Pentagon that the services weren't so committed to compulsory training after all. The American Association of Land-Grant Colleges and State Universities (as it was then known) made a formal inquiry and received a letter from the deputy assistant secretary for manpower of the Department of Defense, with accompanying comments from the Army and Air Force, all of which conveyed an impression of indifference as to whether the universities did or did not require ROTC.

At this, the Land-Grant association, jointly with the State Universities Association (composed of non-Land-Grant universities) and the National Association of State Universities (open to both Land-Grant and non-Land-Grant institutions), demanded a showdown.

A delegation headed by President John A. Hannah of Michigan State University, representing the three associations, appeared before the Defense Department's Armed Forces Policy Board on October 1, 1957. Hannah read a statement which emphasized that "our purpose today is not to argue or to sell; it is rather to learn at first hand from you gentlemen the answers to questions that trouble us, so that we will know better how to plan the work of our universities in the years of great enrollment pressures just ahead of us." After briefly summarizing the group's grievances, Hannah concluded:

We have some simple questions to which we would like

answers—if not today then soon enough that we may use the answers as a basis for planning for the coming year:

In 1957-58 and the years ahead as you see them, is the ROTC program important to the armed services?

If the answer is *no*, we accept the answer and can use the time and space and energy for other purposes.

If the answer is *yes*, we would expect continuous support from the armed services and the Department of Defense, which we think should include:

(1) keeping the long-standing commitment with respect to federally-furnished facilities for military instruction.

(2) consultation on changes in the ROTC programs that affect the role of the colleges and universities in the programs.

(3) vigorous support at all times in our efforts to carry out programs you have devised and which you have asked us to help you carry forward.

Among other things, the group suggested a unified program among all three services.

All that came of this was confirmation that the Department of Defense did not care about required ROTC. Not until late 1962, five years later, did the Department come up with a new program. Representing a compromise between Army and Air Force positions, the plan drew favorable comment from the Land-Grant and State University associations as being "compatible with the educational objectives of the colleges and universities and adequate to assure meeting the qualitative and quanitative officer needs of the respective services."

The outlines of the proposed program emerged in a statement by Defense Secretary Robert McNamara before the House Armed Services Committee. McNamara, in his statement, first conceded that "the college ROTC program . . . has in recent years given rise to increasing dissatisfaction on the part of both the military services and university administrators." Continuing, McNamara said:

Many of the best students find great difficulty in working four years of ROTC courses into their already crowded curricula. Nor is the comparatively small monetary allowance during the junior and senior years much of an inducement. . . .

In many cases, moreover, it is impossible for qualified students . . . to obtain an ROTC commission. A prerequisite for the advanced course is the two-year basic course, which is now available in institutions which enroll only about one third of all male college freshmen. Thus two thirds of the young men entering college will not be eligible to apply for advanced ROTC training.

Even in those schools offering the basic course, only a small percentage are selected for the advanced course. For example, at one large state university, about 5,700 students take the basic course but only about 220 graduates are commissioned each year. The large number of students taking the two-year basic course requires substantial classroom space and a great many regular military personnel to serve as instructors.

McNamara might have pointed out here, as did the Land-Grant association's newsletter in reporting his remarks, that the Defense Department had imposed quotas for advanced ROTC courses and that this was "responsible for the fact that some institutions must turn down qualified advanced course applicants while the program as a whole is not producing enough officers to meet service needs."

McNamara summarized the new ROTC plan as one which would:

(1) Authorize the military departments to offer an elective 2-year ROTC course leading to a commission (which would normally be given in the junior and senior years) in addition to the presently authorized 4-year program. The proposed curriculum would provide a total of 12 to 14 semester hours of on-campus instruction and would permit up to 12 weeks of summer camp training. The new program would initially be used only by the Army and Air Force, and if successful would gradually replace the 4-year program on a school-by-school basis in all except military colleges.

(2) Authorize the military departments to grant a limited number of special scholarships to promising individuals, particularly in the fields of engineering and the physical sciences, provided that they agree to accept a regular commission if tendered and serve four years on active duty. This feature of the plan would be used initially only by the Air Force in an effort to increase the input of technically trained junior officers. If the program proves as successful as we anticipate, the Army may later adopt it.

(3) Authorize an increase in compensation for advanced ROTC students. The rate of compensation for advanced ROTC students has not been increased since 1947.

Despite the hope of a new and happier day generated by the Defense Department's projected solution of the ROTC problem, the realization of this solution was some way off. McNamara's statement was not in the form of proposed legislation; it was simply an informal review of what the Department wanted to do as part of its larger plans for the military establishment. The plan had still to be approved by the Bureau of the Budget, and then and not until then would it be introduced in Congress as legislation, subject to all the uncertainties of any legislation. Even with the Department's new approach, moreover, Land-Grant people were faced with the irretrievable loss of a tradition.

The Land-Grant colleges and universities still have a strong feeling of commitment to help the United States government meet its needs for trained officers, a stronger such commitment than most institutions, and they will continue to be an important element. Nevertheless, the feeling is growing that military training is just something to be shared with all other institutions—and, since the great postwar expansion of the Army and Air Force, there are many others to share it with. As one officer of the Land-Grant association put it in late 1962: "Defense has shown it doesn't really care about past traditions or connections, and this has become somewhat mutual."

Yet, many forward-looking Land-Grant people feel, a new national security role even greater than the one their institutions have played in the training of military officers may be in the offing for them. The fact is that, in both relative and absolute terms, the nation needs fewer officers than was once thought. But those fewer officers need a wider range of qualities and abilities than ever before, and there is opportunity and challenge for Land-Grant colleges and universities to develop them.

Moreover—and every bit as important—there is need for a wide range of talents and capabilities not directly connected with military training at all, in science, in technology, in other areas in which Land-Grant institutions have distinguished themselves through the excellence of their research and graduate work.

Already such Land-Grant institutions as MIT, California, and others have contributed heavily to nuclear development, and already they are involved in the probing of space. If the Land-Grant system is no longer "special" in military training, its foothold in the "mechanic arts" guarantees that it will always be rather special in that area.

Index

Agriculture: degrees awarded by Land-Grant institutions in, 125; instruction at Land-Grant institutions in, 126-132; extension work in, 135-140; research at Land-Grant institutions in, 140-142; training of teachers in, 159. *See also* colleges and universities by name

Aiken, George D., 137

Albrecht, Herbert: on general extension, 17, 19

Alcorn Agricultural and Mechanical College (Miss.): military instruction, 175

Aldrich, Daniel G., Jr.: on role of Land-Grant institution, 11, 146

American Assembly, 14

American Country Life Association: urbanization, 35, 138

Arizona, University of: international affairs, 82

Baty, Harvey: International Study Group III, 40

Bebout, John E., 30

Beggs, W. K., 167

Bennett, Henry Garland, 51

Boelter, L. M. K., 146

Bredemeier, Harry C., 30

Buck, R. Creighton, 149

Caldwell, John T.: Senate testimony on general extension, 18

California, University of: community affairs, 27; international affairs, 78; liberal arts, 105; graduate work, 115, 119, 120, 122, 123; teacher education, 166; ROTC, 179

—Berkeley campus: international affairs, 82, 86; graduate work, 116

—Los Angeles campus: general extension, 10, 20; international affairs, 82, 86; graduate work, 116

Carnegie Corporation, vi, 56

Chambers, Carl C.: on engineering research, 154-156